Diversity and Homogeneity in World Societies

Erika Bourguignon and Lenora S. Greenbaum

HRAF PRESS
1973

About the Authors

Erika Bourguignon is Chairman of the Department of Anthropology at The Ohio State University. She received her B.A. degree from Queens College and her Ph.D. in Anthropology from Northwestern University. During 1963-68 she was the director of the Cross-Cultural Study of Dissociational States, a project conducted at Ohio State with the support of the National Institute of Mental Health. She is the editor of *Religion, Altered States of Consciousness and Social Change*, published by the Ohio State University Press. Her primary research interests are in psychological anthropology and cross-cultural studies.

Lenora Greenbaum is currently teaching in the International Relations Program of the Boston University Overseas Program. She received an A.B. degree from Hunter College, M.A. from New York University, and Ph.D. from The Ohio State University. During 1971-72, she was a Visiting Research Scholar at the Radcliffe Institute in Cambridge, Mass. She has taught at a number of universities including the University of Massachusetts at Boston, The Ohio State University, the University of Virginia, the University of Maryland, and Hunter College. Her areas of special interest and publication include cross-cultural statistical research and African studies.

INTERNATIONAL STANDARD BOOK NUMBER: 0-87536-329-6
LIBRARY OF CONGRESS CATALOG CARD NUMBER: LC 73-86218
© COPYRIGHT 1973
HUMAN RELATIONS AREA FILES, INC.
ALL RIGHTS RESERVED
PRINTED IN THE UNITED STATES OF AMERICA

Contents

iii

List of Charts

List of Tables

Marriage and Kinship

Social Restrictions and Games

Preface

In recent years, cross-cultural and hologeistic studies have expanded in scope and have achieved recognition not only in anthropology but also in related disciplines of the social sciences. Much of this expansion was made possible by the work of George Peter Murdock and the important achievement represented by his *Ethnographic Atlas*, as well as by the program of research and publication undertaken by the Human Relations Area Files.

Because of the interest in and need for consolidation of cross-cultural material, we prepared the forerunner of the present work in 1968, as an Occasional Paper of The Ohio State University Department of Anthropology. This earlier work was entitled *Diversity and Homogeneity*, and subtitled "A Comparative Analysis of Societal Characteristics Based on Data from the *Ethnographic Atlas.*"

Although limited in circulation, the Paper was received warmly by students and teachers alike. Researchers in anthropology as well as such disciplines as sociology and political science found our material useful, as interest in quantification of data and attention to non-Western societies increased in recent years. For these reasons, we were encouraged to prepare an expanded, corrected, and updated version of our original effort.

The major purpose of the present work is to make widely available quantified descriptive data on the large number of societies of the 1967 *Ethnographic Atlas Summary*. The need for a consolidated enumeration of our knowledge of human societies is clear. It is a prerequisite for the development of meaningful generalizations and for the determination of variations and regularities in social organization; in short, a prerequisite for the creation of a science of society.

To quote from Lord Kelvin:

> When you can measure what you are speaking about, and express it in numbers, you know something about it; when you cannot measure it, when you cannot express it in numbers, your knowledge is of a meager and unsatisfactory kind: it may be the beginning of knowledge, but you have scarcely in your thoughts advanced to the stage of science.

The science of society is young indeed when measured by the degree of understanding that can be expressed in numbers. For lack of quantitative information, generalizations have often been based on knowledge of a small number of societies, or a single one, or simply on speculation. Although it is sometimes possible to refute an hypothesis on the basis of a single negative instance, only a large number of cases can provide us with a knowledge of variations and of the conditions under which certain presumed regularities are in fact observable. Undoubtedly, without intensive study of single cases, as in ethnographic fieldwork, there could exist no body of knowledge available for codification and numerical evaluation. Intensive studies of single cases, however, represent a first step. They serve as a basis for broader generalizations only when rigorous enumerations and summarization result.

What has been undertaken here, on the basis of the information provided by the *Ethnographic Atlas*, is an approach to the beginnings of "science" in Lord Kelvin's sense. It is, furthermore, an effort to provide a wealth of descriptive information available for a variety of purposes. As Vallier (1971: 216, 218) has stressed,

> In many fields that fall within the macro-structuralists' range of view, description is underplayed and there is, to use the words of Merton, a "compelling urge to arrive directly at an explanatory idea" . . . Descriptive comparative studies especially should be encouraged and rewarded.

The limitations of the basic data used here are all too well understood by social scientists, certainly by the authors themselves. In our Introduction and throughout this volume, we attempt to specify the limits to the information we now have. We make a claim only for a beginning on which improvement may proceed over a long and tortuous course.

Our thanks are due to the many who have helped and encouraged us. The original tabulations were compiled under the auspices of the Cross-Cultural Study of Dissociational States, at Ohio State, a project supported in full by a grant from the National Institute of Mental Health (MH-07463). Much of the painstaking data preparation for machine processing was done by the staff of that project. Others at Ohio State who were especially helpful to us in the preparation of the original work include Harry Blaine, Simon Dinitz, Irving Greenbaum, Nathan Lazar, and Madge Sanders. The Ohio State University Data Center was most cooperative in processing the material.

For the present book, valuable comments and suggestions were received from Barbara C. Ayres, Harold E. Driver, and John Mogey, among others. Dr. Gunnar Myrdal and Pantheon Books, Inc., kindly gave permission to quote from *Asian Drama*. To Helen Allyn and Paula Lehman of The Ohio State Department of Anthropology go our thanks for typing the final manuscript, to Susan Wolkow for preparing the charts for publication, and to Paul Greenbaum for preparing the machine listing of societies by cluster.

The Radcliffe Institute generously offered its assistance and facilities at critical times in the preparation of this book. The cooperation of Frank W. Moore, Elizabeth P. Swift, and the HRAF Publications Committee were very valuable in completing the book for publication. We are indebted to Mrs. Swift and to her staff for their help in seeing this book through the publication process. And finally, and most important, we wish to express our gratitude to Professor Murdock, without whose monumental *Ethnographic Atlas* our work would not have been possible.

To these and many others along the way, we extend our thanks. The shortcomings of the work, as always, remain our responsibility.

March 14, 1973

Erika Bourguignon
Columbus, Ohio

Lenora Greenbaum
Heidelberg, Germany

Diversity and Homogeneity
in World Societies

I

Introduction

This survey of comparative social organization is presented in the context of two recent tendencies of social science research: the great interest in large-scale, cross-cultural studies among anthropologists and the growing concern with comparative research—in particular comparative research dealing with underdevelopment—among sociologists, economists, and other social scientists. Anthropologists have in recent years become interested in some of the tools, specifically the statistical tools, of the other social sciences; while the latter have been discovering some of the peoples anthropologists have been studying. The materials in this study address themselves to both of these interests.

If we, whatever our professional concerns and competence, wish to make generalizations about human societies, large masses of information seem to be the prime requirement. Until the publication of the *Ethnographic Atlas* (Murdock et al. 1962-ff.; Murdock 1967a, 1967b), no such large quantities of analyzed data were available. David French (1963: 412) has noted wryly that: "anthropologists as a group do not know what they know; they do not know the questions to which they have accumulated the answers." The data of the *Ethnographic Atlas,* presented here in summary form, help us to know what we know, and, perhaps, even what we can know. The impressive growth of cross-cultural studies in the last decade suggests that the existence of such a body of organized data is instrumental in the formulation of significant questions. Thus, by coding and publishing a vast amount of material, on hundreds of human societies the editors of the *Ethnographic Atlas* have performed an unprecedented service, not only to anthropologists but to all social scientists. It now becomes possible by processing and analyzing the data of the *Atlas* to answer a large number of questions about a variety of societal characteristics and their geographic distributions. It is no longer necessary to generalize about family forms, for example—or sex division of labor, or whatever—on the basis of a handful of societies, as unfortunately had to be done in the past; nor is it necessary to base broad generalizations on the special experience of the Western world.

The present volume provides a comprehensive summary of the data available in the *Ethnographic Atlas*. We offer some revisions and consolidations of the *Atlas* codes and as a result are able to present the data of the *Atlas* in readily accessible form. The core of our presentation consists of a series of tables, summarizing the principal statistical data on a variety of societal characteristics for 863 societies in the six major ethnographic regions of the world. By grouping the data by regions, the importance of the differences among them is highlighted. In particular, the dramatic divergencies between the Americas and the Old World are strikingly demonstrated.

In addition to the presentation and discussion of the data and of their implications for research, we include two appendixes, which explain our procedures. Appendix I contains our Code Book and shows in full detail how it is based on—and how it differs from—the Code Book of the *Ethnographic Atlas*. Appendix II is a print-out of our card file, providing a complete listing of the societies and of the data coded for each.

The *Ethnographic Atlas* is a comprehensive catalog of a variety of characteristics of human societies. As such, its research potential is enormous. At the same time, its limitations must be clearly understood in order to employ what it has to offer to best advantage. Therefore, before proceeding to a presentation of the data and in order to permit the reader an evaluation of the materials that follow, it is necessary to comment on the nature of the basic data of the *Ethnographic Atlas* in some detail. Only in this way can their potential be clearly understood.

Sources

The sources used in assembling the coded data of the *Ethnographic Atlas* were, according to Murdock (1967a: 109), "practically the entire ethnographic literature" for sub-Saharan Africa, North and South America, North Africa, the Semitic Near East, Assam and Burma, Micronesia, and Polynesia. For the remainder of the world, "only a reasonably wide and representative selection of societies" is included (Murdock 1967a: 109-10). Furthermore, the literature surveyed included publications in seven European languages (English, French, German, Spanish, Dutch, Italian, and Portuguese), as well as others in translation. Sources ranged from reconstructions by historians of three societies in antiquity, to the records of explorers and missionaries, to current writings by anthropologists, including unpublished communications from colleagues recently returned from the field. The time spread of the societies covered is reviewed below. It is clear that the several thousand sources consulted vary not only in details of coverage but also in theoretical preoccupations, biases, standards of accuracy, etc.

Although in the past anthropologists, with their emphasis on field work and first-hand data, have done little to develop a critical approach to sources, two contemporary anthropologists have made important contributions in this area, although in characteristically different ways.

Evans-Pritchard (1971) strongly condemns the uncritical use of sources by anthropologists in general and by comparativists in particular, whose work he sees vitiated as a result. He presents a detailed critique of a number of sources concerning the Sudan, on the basis of his own field work and of his intimate knowledge of the area. He does so by citing a large number of specific statements and refuting them in some detail.

Raoul Naroll, on the other hand, is concerned with what he calls "quality control": the reliability of the data taken from a variety of sources for purposes of comparative analysis. He has dealt with this problem a number of times (Naroll 1962, 1970a; Naroll et al. 1970). With a group of co-workers (Naroll et al. 1970), he offers a list of control factors or selection standards to be met by ethnographic sources. These are: twelve months of fieldwork, knowledge of the native language, and a minimum of forty pages of total report, with no less than two pages each devoted to each of ten or more of the seventy-nine topics listed in the *Outline of Cultural Materials* (Murdock et al. 1969). Limiting himself to "primitive tribes," i.e. societies having no native written literature and, in most cases, no traditional cities of over

50,000, and based on his control factors, he arrives at a Standard Ethnographic Sample of 224 societies.

The 863 societies used in this book, however, represent a selection by Murdock from a larger group of over 1,100 previously coded in the twenty-one installments of the *Ethnographic Atlas*. Thus, more than a fourth of the original number were omitted. The important criteria for selection here were the quality of the sources and the completeness of the data available, as well as broad representation of varying cultural clusters (Murdock 1967a: 109). Specific details of these criteria are, however, not indicated.

Concept of "Society"

While the problem of the definition of the societal unit has been aired (Naroll 1964, Köbben 1967, Naroll 1970b), no universally satisfactory solution is available. In the *Atlas,* the basic units tend to be societies as described in ethnographic monographs, accounts of missionaries, administrators, travelers, and others. In general, the descriptions of a particular local group or community are applied to a larger population which shares common features of social life and culture with the specific group studied. The majority of societies are simple and nonindustrial. There are, however, a number of complex societies included. The coverage of industrial societies remains minimal, only 14 out of 863. Like the simple societies, the industrial as well as the nonindustrial complex societies are generally represented by reports on small village communities, rather than by studies of towns or cities. While this makes for greater comparability with villages among all peoples, it probably tends to underemphasize some of the characteristic and distinctive features of complex societies.

Population Size

Some idea of the nature of the societies studied here can be obtained from data on population size (Table A). Population estimates are included in the *Ethnographic Atlas* for 655 of the 863 societies, i.e. for more than 75% of the total number. This percentage varies from region to region. The most complete information is furnished for Africa (91% with population data). On the other hand, in the Circum-Mediterranean and South

Population	Total		Sub-Saharan Africa		Circum-Mediterranean		East Eurasia		Insular Pacific		North America		South America	
	No.	%	No.	%	No.	%	No.	%	No.	%	No.	%	No.	%
Total	**863**		**238**		**96**		**94**		**127**		**219**		**89**	
No. without information	208	24	21	9	35	36	21	22	35	27	71	32	25	36
% without information														
Total with information	**655**	**100**	**217**	**100**	**61**	**100**	**73**	**100**	**92**	**100**	**148**	**100**	**64**	**100**
Less than 100	9	1	-	-	-	-	-	-	1	1	6	4	2	3
100-less than 1,000	125	19	3	1	3	5	4	5	18	20	81	55	16	25
1,000-less than 10,000	160	24	17	8	9	15	12	17	41	45	49	33	32	50
10,000-less than 100,000	170	26	94	44	16	26	20	27	22	24	9	6	9	14
100,000-less than one million	142	22	93	43	20	33	19	26	4	4	3	2	3	5
One million-less than ten million	41	6	10	5	12	20	12	17	5	5	-	-	2	3
Ten million and over	8	-	-	-	1	2	6	8	1	1	-	-	-	-
Total population in millions	393		49		75		213		47		1		8	

American areas, population figures are available for less than two-thirds of all societies. It must be kept in mind that the population figures are merely general estimates and cannot be relied upon for precise accuracy. In a few cases, they represent the population of the village studied, and in most cases that of the larger society of which the village is a part. The figures at best can only provide us with some general indication of the comparative sizes of the groups involved.

The total population for the 655 societies for which this information is available is about 393 million people (about 10% of the current world population). Of this number, 213 million, or more than one-half, are accounted for by the large populations of East Eurasia. At the other extreme, the indigenous tribes of North America account for only one million people. The rather low population figure for the Circum-Mediterranean area (75 million) indicates that the large populations of western Europe and the industrialized Western Hemisphere are largely omitted from the *Atlas*. As further evidence, only one society in this area is shown as having a population of 10 million or more.

The distribution of all societies by size of population shows almost 75% falling in population ranges between one thousand and one million people. This varies, however, among the geographic regions. East Eurasia and the Circum-Mediterranean have the largest populations and in each, 70% or more of the societies have populations between ten thousand and ten million. In North and South America, 75% or more of the societies have populations between one hundred and ten thousand. At the extremes in populations figures, 55% of the North American societies are in the one hundred to one thousand group, whereas 25% of the East Eurasian societies have over one million people, 8% having over ten million people.

The available population figures do not always date from the time of the ethnographic study used for *Atlas* coding. In many cases, population figures are of a later date than that of the field investigation. This is indicated in each case in Appendix II. Furthermore, these population figures do not reflect the so-called "population explosion" of recent years.

Table B: Date of Observation of Societies Within Each Major Ethnographic Region

Date of Observation	Total No.	Total %	Sub-Saharan Africa No.	Circum-Mediterranean No.	East Eurasia No.	Insular Pacific No.	North America No.	South America No.
Total	**863**	**100**	**238**	**96**	**94**	**127**	**219**	**89**
20th century	591	68	220	78	83	108	33	69
Second half of 19th century	217	25	14	12	9	11	161	10
First half of 19th century	18	3	2	-	1	7	7	1
16th through 18th century	24	3	-	1	-	-	17	6
First through 15th century	1	-	-	1	-	-	-	-
B.C.	3	-	-	3	-	-	-	-
No date	9	1	2	1	1	1	1	3

Time of Observation

In considering the population figures, as well as all the other data of the *Atlas*, a clear idea of the time of observation of these societies must be kept in mind (Table B). The basic source materials used for determining *Atlas* codes range in time from antiquity to 1960 A.D. The three ancient societies are Ancient Egypt (1400 B.C.), Babylonia (2000 B.C.), and Hebrews (800 B.C.). With the exception of the Icelanders of the eleventh century, no other description precedes the period of European explorations. Most societies (93%) have been observed and described since 1850, and data for almost 70% of all societies are based on twentieth-century studies. In all areas, there are a very few societies from earlier times. The data on the African, East Eurasian, and Insular Pacific areas tend to be the most current, representing much recent anthropological work. Descriptions of North American indigenous societies concentrate very heavily on the state of these societies in the nineteenth century.

Totality versus Sampling

The 863 societies are to be construed as a *totality* of societies, as an "encyclopedia of classified ethnographic information" (Murdock et al. 1962: 114), and not a *sample* of human societies. This is in sharp contrast to the "World Ethnographic Sample," the societies of which were selected on the basis of specified criteria (Murdock 1957), and which, as its name implies, was designed as a sample of world societies. On the other hand, the 863 societies of the *Atlas* are covered by the inclusive phrase, the "known cultural universe" (Murdock 1967a: 115). This "universe" actually refers more to cultural types or clusters than to individual "culture bearing units" or societies. All 863 societies, however, are assigned to one of the 412 cultural clusters designated by Murdock; most clusters are represented by only one society, but for many, data on two or more are provided. (See Appendix II, The Ohio State University Punched Card File of Ethnographic Data: Listing of Sample Societies by Cluster.) The "known cultural universe" is described as consisting of *"all societies and clusters whose cultures have been adequately described without arbitrary limitations of time, area, or the*

languages in which the ethnographic accounts have been written"
(Murdock 1967a: 113). The availability of "adequately described" societies is, of course, an obstacle in any desire for
completeness and is discussed further below. The emphasis of
the *Ethnographic Atlas* is on the *variety* of known types of societies, rather than on representativeness or simultaneity. It is all
the more interesting, in view of this emphasis on variety, that
the six major areas of the world nevertheless exhibit marked
individual patterns of societal characteristics.

General Reliability

Two additional factors affect the reliability of the data presented here: the quality and extent of the ethnographic literature,
i.e. (1) which particular societies have been selected for study
by ethnographers and others and their competence in observing
and recording societal features; and (2) the selection of sources
by the editors and the consistency of coding for the *Ethnographic
Atlas*. The latter has been discussed at some length by Murdock
(1967a: 109-10).

The very availability and completeness of sources appears to
be a severely limiting factor. Consequently, it should be noted
that data on all variables are not available for all of the 863 societies included in the tabulations. Available information varies
from 100% to only a small proportion of cases in some instances.
(This is discussed more fully in the next section.) It is clear that
observers have very disproportionately emphasized certain kinds
of information and ignored other kinds to a considerable extent.
Furthermore, many societies, especially the complex, industrial
ones, lack the adequate anthropological treatment that would
permit their inclusion in the *Ethnographic Atlas*.

In spite of all these reservations, however, there are indications
of reliability of the data that are available: (a) For many societies,
the work of several observers has been consulted to determine the
Ethnographic Atlas coding, which reduces the influence of bias;
(b) characteristic patterns peculiar to particular ethnographic
areas were found—as will be described later on—which lends further support to the probable soundness of much of the basic
information. This means that different observers, examining
different societies within the same broad ethnographic region,

have come to describe economic, political, and/or social phenomena that are generally shared by them.

We hope to be able to demonstrate the great potential usefulness of these materials, in spite of the limitations imposed at present by a lack of refinement or completeness in the raw data.

II

A Survey of Societal Characteristics

The following detailed summary of the incidence and distribution of societal characteristics of 863 societies from all parts of the world covers selected features of each society's economy; particular aspects of social, political, and kinship organization; and some details of religious belief, social restrictions, and games. Our statistical tabulations are based on the coded data for all 863 societies published in the revised summary of the *Ethnographic Atlas* (Murdock 1967a).

These data are organized, for comparative purposes, into six major world areas, according to the geographic location of the societies. The six major world areas are defined in the *Ethnographic Atlas* (1967a: 154) as follows:

A Africa, exclusive of Madagascar and the northern and northeastern portions of the continent.

C Circum-Mediterranean, including Europe, Turkey and the Caucasus, the Semitic Near East, and northern and northeastern Africa.

E East Eurasia, excluding Formosa, the Philippines, Indonesia, and the area assigned to the Circum-Mediterranean but including Madagascar and other islands in the Indian Ocean.

I Insular Pacific, embracing all of Oceania as well as areas like Australia, Indonesia, Formosa, and the Philippines that are not always included therewith.

N North America, including the indigenous societies of this continent as far south as the Isthmus of Tehuantepec.

S South America, including the Antilles, Yucatan, and Central America as well as the continent itself.

Each of these major areas is subdivided in the *Ethnographic Atlas* into ten lesser regions. The Circum-Mediterranean area includes Overseas Europeans among its lesser regions. (For details, see Appendix I, the OSU Code Book.)

The major areas are represented by varying numbers of societies, and the resulting distribution is shown below in descending numerical order.*

Total	*863*
Africa (sub-Saharan)	238
North America	219
Insular Pacific	127
Circum-Mediterranean	96
East Eurasia	94
South America	89

*There is a small discrepancy between these figures and those published in the *Ethnographic Atlas* (Murdock 1967a: 109). Our figures here represent an actual count of the societies listed in the April 1967 issue of the *Ethnographic Atlas* (Murdock 1967a) for each ethnographic region.

Revision of Atlas Data

While our basic source material is the coded data of the *Ethnographic Atlas* as prepared by Professor Murdock and his associates (Murdock 1967a: 110), we have, nevertheless, omitted some categories and revised and combined most of those we have retained, thus consolidating the materials of the *Atlas* into the form used here (Appendix I, Code Book). The categories we chose and the groupings we used in our revision were intended for general research use. We have, however, made no codings ourselves from additional published sources or field studies, nor have we added any societies to those included in the *Atlas*.

The effects of our revisions are twofold: first, for almost all societal characteristics, our categories are fewer in number than those of the *Atlas*, and, therefore, statistical frequencies are larger for each category. This revision was felt to be desirable, since we wanted to be able to make generalizations about large numbers of societies. To the extent that the categories of the

Atlas are more refined, each covers fewer societies and permits consideration of types with limited incidence. The great variety of types of cousin marriage and residence rules specified in the *Atlas* are examples of this. Our consolidation of categories results in a spread of the 863 societies over an average of four possible alternatives for most societal characteristics. We have avoided, whenever possible, polarizing the data into dichotomies, and likewise we have avoided retaining eight or ten possible alternative conditions where meaningful combinations could be made. Our tables on subsistence economy, for example, indicate the dependence of a society on a particular activity (e.g. agriculture) for 0 to 25%, or 26 to 45%, or 46 to 75%, or 76 to 100% of its subsistence. This is in sharp contrast to the ten *Atlas* categories, eight of which account for a 10% range each in subsistence dependence, one for a 5% range, and one for a 15% range. We believe that combining these categories into four larger groups gives a more uniform and more concise picture of the range of subsistence economy dependence. All consolidations for individual societal characteristics are of this type.

Second, by combining the codes of some societal characteristics or by separating information on characteristics which have been coded together in the *Atlas,* we have provided information not otherwise directly accessible, as indicated in the following examples:

In the important question of subsistence economy, we combined the codes in two ways: (1) The codes for dependence on gathering, hunting, and fishing have been added together for each society and a new code provided, showing the degree of dependence on this combination; and (2) the codes for dependence on animal husbandry and on agriculture have been examined for each society and a new code established, showing whether or not the society depends substantially on each of these activities. The advantage of these combinations is that they give a clearer picture of subsistence economy. As shown in Tables 2, and 3, in all areas of the world, few societies get more than one-half of their subsistence from gathering or hunting or fishing. When these codes are combined, however, as shown in Table the we find that a number of societies depend rather heavily on the combination, and we can see, moreover, the geographical area in which this dependence is greatest (in North and South Amer-

ica), and where it is least (in the Circum-Mediterranean and
Africa). Similarly, in Table 7, the Circum-Mediterranean stands
out as the only area with substantial subsistence economy dependence on a combination of agriculture and animal husbandry.
These data, we feel, provide greater insights into subsistence
economy than a reliance on the data of Tables 1 to 5 alone. These
groupings, of course, should not lead one to overlook the fact that
many societies have subsistence economies of a mixed type, i.e.
that they may combine, for example, agriculture with hunting in
significant proportions.

By separating the data contained in the *Atlas* Columns 14 or
15, on marriage and family forms, we are able to provide one
table on the forms of marriage (Table 27) and a separate one on
forms of the family (Table 28). It is also possible to develop
tables on each family form, showing the incidence of marriage
forms for each, and, conversely, tables for each marriage form,
showing the distribution of family forms.

We have coded levels of technology independent of sex division
of labor, and are thus able to show the numerical distribution of
craft specialization (Table 16) and industrial specialization (Table
17) among the 863 societies. This information is not easily deter-
minable in the *Atlas* material.

By combining all data on kin groups into one column, we can
present the distribution of kin groups for all 863 societies. This
again cannot be easily done from the *Atlas* without carefully
identifying those societies with double descent (coded in the
Atlas both for patrilineal and matrilineal descent), as we have
had to do.

In respect to sex division of labor, jurisdictional hierarchy,
and class stratification, our codes permit a variety of analyses
beyond what is included here.

The coding consolidations that we present are, we believe, ad-
vantageous to cross-cultural research. As Driver and Schuessler
point out (1967: 347): "Experience has shown that in the long
run the splitting of data into more and more categories of lower
and lower frequency tends to depress correlations to the point
where many of them fail to meet a test of significance, because
the error variance increases relative to the total variance." By
making these changes in the coding categories and rearranging

the data in the several ways indicated, we have sought to increase the usefulness of the coded information for research purposes. We feel that the various coding revisions and consolidations make accessible aspects of the data that are not otherwise readily apparent.

We wish to make no general claim for the superiority of our categories over those of the *Atlas,* but only for their appropriateness for certain types of research problems. The tables we present summarize the major features of the 863 coded societies. They exploit some, but not all, the advantages of our coding. Furthermore, they serve to illustrate the particular uses to which this coding can be put. Other, and more refined, analyses are possible, dealing with one or more particular world areas or with particular subjects.

Statistical Findings

In discussing the material presented in the tabulations, we have grouped our findings under four general headings: Economy (covering Tables 1 through 17), Social Structure, Political Organization, and Religion (Tables 18 through 24), Marriage and Kinship (Tables 25 through 32), and Social Restrictions and Games (Tables 33 through 37).

The number of societies represented in each table varies considerably. Under Economy, data indicating the degree of dependence on various types of subsistence activities are available for all 863 societies. The number of societies, however, for which information is available on sex division of labor in subsistence activities ranges from 398 (Sex Division of Labor in Gathering) to 639 (Sex Division of Labor in Agriculture). This reflects both the number of societies in which these subsistence activities are present and important and the number of societies for which data on the division of labor by sex are available. With respect to Social Structure, Political Organization, and Religion, all 863 societies have a recorded settlement pattern; while the number of societies with data for other characteristics under this general heading ranges from 465 (Mean Size of the Local Community) to 774 (Stratification of Freemen). Data on Kinship and Marriage are available for more than 850 societies, with the exception of Community Organization (793 societies) and Cousin Marriage (762 societies). In regard to social restrictions, the coverage of societies ranges from 304 (Postpartum Sex Taboo) to 815 (Male Genital Mutilations). Information on games covers only 391 societies, less than one-half of the 863 societies. (In the tables that follow, the frequencies and percentages refer only to those societies for which information on the particular societal characteristic is available.)

These figures give some indication of the lack of uniformity to be found in the ethnographic sources and point to the need for a basic, uniform standard of desirable information for field work, which all ethnographers could adhere to, no matter what additional special subjects they might choose to study.

Some of the more striking findings in the tables are discussed below, as a help to the reader in finding his way through the large number of statistical tabulations. The volume of detailed information and of interesting comparisons among the six ethnographic regions included in these tables is large indeed and goes far beyond the salient features mentioned.

Economy (Tables 1-17)

In this section we present tables on subsistence activities and their relative importance in the various world regions. This importance is indicated in Tables 1-7 by an estimate of the degree of dependence on a particular activity. These are followed by two tables (8-9) dealing with the distribution of type and intensity of agriculture and of the type of animal husbandry. The next group of tables (10-14) deals with sex division of labor in the several subsistence activities. Table 15 then presents an overall summary of data on the distribution of subsistence activities, as revealed in Columns 21-25, which provide the coded data on sex division of labor. It should be noted that information on sex division of labor is available on a smaller total number of societies than data on the relative dependence on the several subsistence economies. Therefore, the figures given in Table 15 are smaller than those in Tables 1-7. However, the numbers of societies indicated as having the given subsistence activities are those also for which sex division of labor is shown in Tables 10-14.

Table 1: Degree of Dependence on Gathering
(Column 12)

Code	Percentage of Dependence	Total		Sub-Saharan Africa		Circum-Mediterranean		East Eurasia		Insular Pacific		North America		South America	
		No.	%	No.	%	No.	%	No.	%	No.	%	No.	%	No.	%
	Total	**863**	**100**	**238**	**100**	**96**	**100**	**94**	**100**	**127**	**100**	**219**	**100**	**89**	**100**
1	0 - 25%	730	85	233	98	96	100	90	96	112	88	124	57	75	84
2	26% - 45%	85	10	1	-	-	-	3	3	11	9	58	26	12	13
3	46% - 75%	46	5	3	1	-	-	-	-	4	3	37	17	2	2
4	76% - 100%	2	-	1	-	-	-	1	1	-	-	-	-	-	-

Table 2: Degree of Dependence on Hunting
(Column 13)

Code	Percentage of Dependence	Total		Sub-Saharan Africa		Circum-Mediterranean		East Eurasia		Insular Pacific		North America		South America	
		No.	%	No.	%	No.	%	No.	%	No.	%	No.	%	No.	%
	Total	**863**	**100**	**238**	**100**	**96**	**100**	**94**	**100**	**127**	**100**	**219**	**100**	**89**	**100**
1	0 - 25%	662	77	229	96	96	100	85	90	117	92	73	33	62	70
2	26% - 45%	151	18	7	3	-	-	8	9	9	7	108	49	19	21
3	46% - 75%	38	4	2	1	-	-	1	1	1	1	26	12	8	9
4	76% - 100%	12	1	-	-	-	-	-	-	-	-	12	6	-	-

Table 3: Degree of Dependence on Fishing
(Column 14)

Code	Percentage of Dependence	Total		Sub-Saharan Africa		Circum-Mediterranean		East Eurasia		Insular Pacific		North America		South America	
		No.	%	No.	%	No.	%	No.	%	No.	%	No.	%	No.	%
	Total	863	100	238	100	96	100	94	100	127	100	219	100	89	100
1	0 - 25%	644	75	218	92	92	96	81	86	70	55	120	55	63	71
2	26% - 45%	139	16	16	7	4	4	9	10	43	34	46	21	21	24
3	46% - 75%	73	8	4	2	-	-	3	3	12	9	49	22	5	6
4	76% - 100%	7	1	-	-	-	-	1	1	2	2	4	2	-	-

Table 4: Degree of Dependence on Animal Husbandry
(Column 15)

Code	Percentage of Dependence	Total		Sub-Saharan Africa		Circum-Mediterranean		East Eurasia		Insular Pacific		North America		South America	
		No.	%	No.	%	No.	%	No.	%	No.	%	No.	%	No.	%
	Total	**863**	**100**	**238**	**100**	**96**	**100**	**94**	**100**	**127**	**100**	**219**	**100**	**89**	**100**
1	0 - 25%	688	80	175	74	23	24	63	67	124	98	216	99	87	98
2	26% - 45%	130	15	51	21	51	53	21	22	3	2	3	1	1	1
3	46% - 75%	29	3	11	5	13	14	4	4	-	-	-	-	1	1
4	76% - 100%	16	2	1	-	9	9	6	6	-	-	-	-	-	-

Table 5: Degree of Dependence on Agriculture
(Column 16)

Code	Percentage of Dependence	Total		Sub-Saharan Africa		Circum-Mediterranean		East Eurasia		Insular Pacific		North America		South America	
		No.	%	No.	%	No.	%	No.	%	No.	%	No.	%	No.	%
	Total	**863**	**100**	**238**	**100**	**96**	**100**	**94**	**100**	**127**	**100**	**219**	**100**	**89**	**100**
1	0 - 25%	249	29	12	5	16	17	21	22	14	11	162	74	24	27
2	26% - 45%	86	10	19	8	8	8	4	4	14	11	19	9	22	25
3	46% - 75%	490	57	190	80	68	71	64	68	98	77	31	14	39	44
4	76% - 100%	38	4	17	7	4	4	5	5	1	1	7	3	4	4

Table 6: Degree of Dependence on Gathering, Hunting, and Fishing Combined
(Column 17)

Code	Degree of Dependence	Total		Sub-Saharan Africa		Circum-Mediterranean		East Eurasia		Insular Pacific		North America		South America	
		No.	%	No.	%	No.	%	No.	%	No.	%	No.	%	No.	%
	Total	**863**	**100**	**238**	**100**	**96**	**100**	**94**	**100**	**127**	**100**	**219**	**100**	**89**	**100**
1	Low dependence	343	40	140	59	90	94	58	62	29	23	16	7	10	11
2	Moderately low dependence	192	22	81	34	3	3	21	22	60	47	10	5	17	19
3	Moderately heavy dependence	99	12	8	3	3	3	3	3	23	18	25	11	37	42
4	Heavy dependence	229	26	9	4	-	-	12	13	15	12	168	77	25	28

Table 7: Degree of Dependence on Animal Husbandry and Agriculture Combined
(Column 18)

Code	Degree of Dependence	Total		Sub-Saharan Africa		Circum-Mediterranean		East Eurasia		Insular Pacific		North America		South America	
		No.	%	No.	%	No.	%	No.	%	No.	%	No.	%	No.	%
	Total	**863**	**100**	**238**	**100**	**96**	**100**	**94**	**100**	**127**	**100**	**219**	**100**	**89**	**100**
1	Societies get *more than* one-quarter of their subsistence from animal husbandry and more than one-quarter from agriculture.	144	17	60	25	57	59	20	21	3	2	3	1	1	1
2	Societies get *less than* one-quarter of their subsistence from animal husbandry and/or less than one-quarter from agriculture.	719	83	178	75	39	41	74	79	124	98	216	99	88	99

Table 8: Type and Intensity of Agriculture
(Column 19)

Code	Type	Total		Sub-Saharan Africa		Circum-Mediterranean		East Eurasia		Insular Pacific		North America		South America	
		No.	%	No.	%	No.	%	No.	%	No.	%	No.	%	No.	%
	Total	**863**	**100**	**238**	**100**	**96**	**100**	**94**	**100**	**127**	**100**	**219**	**100**	**89**	**100**
1	Casual agriculture	29	3	-	-	5	5	6	6	1	1	9	4	8	9
2	Shifting agriculture	328	38	170	71	13	14	28	30	22	17	33	15	62	70
3	Horticulture	84	10	-	-	-	-	1	1	80	63	-	-	3	3
4	Intensive agriculture	236	27	60	25	75	78	47	50	16	13	32	15	6	7
5	Complete absence of agriculture	186	22	8	3	3	3	12	13	8	6	145	66	10	11

Table 9: Type of Animal Husbandry
(Column 20)

Code	Kinds of Animals Herded	Total		Sub-Saharan Africa		Circum-Mediterranean		East Eurasia		Insular Pacific		North America		South America	
		No.	%	No.	%	No.	%	No.	%	No.	%	No.	%	No.	%
	Total	**859**	**100**	**238**	**100**	**95**	**100**	**94**	**100**	**127**	**100**	**217**	**100**	**88**	**100**
1	Bovine animals	315	37	132	56	78	82	75	80	17	13	7	3	6	7
2	Equine animals	72	8	-	-	14	15	1	1	-	-	51	24	6	7
3	Deer	7	1	1	-	1	1	5	5	-	-	1	-	-	-
4	Pigs	98	11	1	-	-	-	2	2	84	66	1	-	10	11
5	Sheep and goats	107	12	91	38	2	2	2	2	3	2	6	3	3	3
6	Absence of animal husbandry	260	30	14	6	-	-	9	10	23	18	151	70	63	72

Table 10: Sex Division of Labor in Gathering
(Column 21)

Sex Division of Labor Where Gathering Is Present:

Code	Division of Labor	Total		Sub-Saharan Africa		Circum-Mediterranean		East Eurasia		Insular Pacific		North America		South America	
		No.	%	No.	%	No.	%	No.	%	No.	%	No.	%	No.	%
	Total	**398**	**100**	**81**	**100**	**15**	**100**	**37**	**100**	**47**	**100**	**160**	**100**	**58**	**100**
1,5	Equal participation of both sexes	56	14	11	14	1	7	8	22	14	30	9	6	13	22
2,6	Women perform the activity alone or do appreciably more than men.	310	78	61	75	12	80	28	76	19	40	149	93	41	71
3,7	Men perform the activity alone or do appreciably more than women.	32	8	9	11	2	13	1	3	14	30	2	1	4	7

Table 11: Sex Division of Labor in Hunting
(Column 22)

Sex Division of Labor Where Hunting Is Present:

Code	Division of Labor	Total		Sub-Saharan Africa		Circum-Mediterranean		East Eurasia		Insular Pacific		North America		South America	
		No.	%	No.	%	No.	%	No.	%	No.	%	No.	%	No.	%
	Total	**741**	**100**	**216**	**100**	**68**	**100**	**72**	**100**	**81**	**100**	**218**	**100**	**86**	**100**
1,5	Equal participation of both sexes	-	-	-	-	-	-	-	-	-	-	-	-	-	-
2,6	Women perform the activity alone or do appreciably more than men.	-	-	-	-	-	-	-	-	-	-	-	-	-	-
3,7	Men perform the activity alone or do appreciably more than women.	741	100	216	100	68	100	72	100	81	100	218	100	86	100

Table 12: Sex Division of Labor in Fishing
(Column 23)

Sex Division of Labor Where Fishing Is Present:

Code	Division of Labor	Total		Sub-Saharan Africa		Circum-Mediterranean		East Eurasia		Insular Pacific		North America		South America	
		No.	*%*	*No.*	*%*	*No.*	*%*	*No.*	*%*	*No.*	*%*	*No.*	*%*	*No.*	*%*
	Total	**564**	**100**	**142**	**100**	**36**	**100**	**68**	**100**	**102**	**100**	**142**	**100**	**74**	**100**
1,5	Equal participation of both sexes	83	15	24	17	3	8	14	21	28	27	8	6	6	8
2,6	Women perform the activity alone or do appreciably more than men.	36	6	21	15	1	3	4	6	9	9	1	1	-	-
3,7	Men perform the activity alone or do appreciably more than women.	444	79	97	68	32	89	50	73	65	64	132	93	68	92
8	Sex not specified	1	-	-	-	-	-	-	-	-	-	1	1	-	-

Table 13: Sex Division of Labor in Animal Husbandry
(Column 24)

Societies Where Animal Husbandry Is Present:

Code	Division of Labor	Total		Sub-Saharan Africa		Circum-Mediterranean		East Eurasia		Insular Pacific		North America		South America	
		No.	%	No.	%	No.	%	No.	%	No.	%	No.	%	No.	%
	Total	**413**	**100**	**136**	**100**	**80**	**100**	**72**	**100**	**60**	**100**	**47**	**100**	**18**	**100**
1,5	Equal participation of the sexes	92	22	25	18	24	30	21	29	11	18	6	13	5	28
2,6	Women perform the activity alone or do appreciably more than men.	57	14	5	4	5	6	6	8	33	55	3	6	5	28
3,7	Men perform the activity alone or do appreciably more than women.	263	64	106	78	51	64	45	62	16	27	37	79	8	44
8	Sex not specified	1	-	-	-	-	-	-	-	-	-	1	2	-	-

Table 14: Sex Division of Labor in Agriculture
(Column 25)

Sex Division of Labor Where Agriculture Is Present:

Code	Division of Labor	Total		Sub-Saharan Africa		Circum-Mediterranean		East Eurasia		Insular Pacific		North America		South America	
		No.	*%*	*No.*	*%*	*No.*	*%*	*No.*	*%*	*No.*	*%*	*No.*	*%*	*No.*	*%*
	Total	**639**	**100**	**223**	**100**	**80**	**100**	**81**	**100**	**111**	**100**	**69**	**100**	**75**	**100**
1,5	Equal participation of both sexes	203	32	59	26	22	27	43	53	46	41	11	16	22	29
2,6	Women perform the activity alone or do appreciably more than men.	232	36	122	55	3	4	8	10	38	34	29	42	32	43
3,7	Men perform the activity alone or do appreciably more than women.	204	32	42	19	55	69	30	37	27	24	29	42	21	28

(Column 21-25)

Code	Subsistence Activity	Total		Sub-Saharan Africa		Circum-Mediterranean		East Eurasia		Insular Pacific		North America		South America	
		No.	%	No.	%	No.	%	No.	%	No.	%	No.	%	No.	%
1-6	**Gathering** (Col. 21)	545	100	113	100	45	100	76	100	82	100	168	100	61	100
	Present	398	73	81	72	15	33	37	49	47	57	160	95	58	95
9	Absent or unimportant	147	27	32	28	30	67	39	51	35	43	8	5	3	5
1-6	**Hunting** (Col. 22)	816	100	221	100	84	100	90	100	116	100	219	100	86	100
	Present	741	91	216	98	68	81	72	80	81	70	218	99	86	100
9	Absent or unimportant	75	9	5	2	16	19	18	20	35	30	1	1	-	-
1,2,3, 5,6,7,	**Fishing** (Col. 23)	717	100	187	100	74	100	88	100	111	100	180	100	77	100
	Present	564	79	142	75	36	49	68	77	102	92	142	79	74	96
9	Absent or unimportant	153	21	45	24	38	51	20	23	9	8	38	21	3	4
1-7	**Animal Husbandry** (Col. 24)	671	100	147	100	80	100	81	100	84	100	200	100	79	100
	Present	413	62	136	92	80	100	72	89	60	71	47	24	18	23
9	Absent or unimportant	258	38	11	8	-	-	9	11	24	29	153	76	61	77
1-7	**Agriculture** (Col. 25)	827	100	231	100	84	100	93	100	120	100	214	100	85	100
	Present	639	77	223	96	80	95	81	87	111	92	69	32	75	88
9	Absent or unimportant	188	23	8	4	4	5	12	13	9	8	145	68	10	12

*(among societies for which information on sex division of labor is available)

Table 16: Craft Specialization
(Column 26)

Code	Societies with Craft Specialization	Total		Sub-Saharan Africa		Circum-Mediterranean		East Eurasia		Insular Pacific		North America		South America	
		No.	%	No.	%	No.	%	No.	%	No.	%	No.	%	No.	%
	Total Societies	**863**		**238**		**96**		**94**		**127**		**219**		**89**	
	Societies with craft specialization	371	41	169	71	83	86	67	71	42	33	7	3	3	3
	Number of Crafts per society														
	Total	**371**	**100**	**169**	**100**	**83**	**100**	**67**	**100**	**42**	**100**	**7**	-	**3**	-
1	One craft	267	72	137	81	45	54	40	60	37	88	5	-	3	-
2	Two crafts	57	15	18	11	18	22	15	22	5	12	1	-	-	-
3	Three crafts	31	8	11	6	13	16	7	10	-	-	-	-	-	-
4	Four crafts	9	2	2	1	4	5	3	5	-	-	-	-	-	-

Table 17: Industrial Specialization
(Column 27)

Code	Number of Industries in Industrial Societies	Total	Circum-Mediterranean	East Eurasia
	Total	**14**	**13**	**1**
1	One industry	6	6	-
2	Two industries	4	3	1
3	Three industries	3	3	-
4	Four industries	1	1	-

Agriculture represents the most important source of subsistence economy in most of the world. In Africa, 87% of the societies depend upon agriculture for one-half or more of their subsistence. In the Circum-Mediterranean, East Eurasian, and Insular Pacific areas, between 70% and 80% of the societies obtain most of their subsistence from agriculture, while in South America, only 48% of the societies do so. North American indigenous societies are least dependent on agriculture, with almost 75% obtaining less than one-quarter of their subsistence in this way.

While shifting agriculture tends to predominate in Africa and South America, in the Circum-Mediterranean area intensive agriculture characterizes most societies. In East Eurasia intensive agriculture is found in one-half the societies, with shifting agriculture present in another 30% of the societies. Horticulture is frequent only in the Insular Pacific area (present among 63% of the societies). Although North American indigenous societies as a whole have little agriculture, 15% of the societies are classified as having intensive agriculture and 15% shifting agriculture. (Here it should be remembered that North America as defined in the *Atlas* has its southern limit at the Isthmus of Tehuantepec.)

Animal husbandry is a secondary subsistence activity among African, Circum-Mediterranean, and East Eurasian societies. Among the Insular Pacific, North American, and South American societies, animal husbandry is minimal or nonexistent. In the Circum-Mediterranean area, 60% of all societies depend substantially on both animal husbandry and agriculture. This is the only ethnographic region in which heavy dependence on this combination is widespread.

Cattle are the predominant type of animal herded in Africa, the Circum-Mediterranean, and East Eurasia. In Africa, sheep and goats are second in importance. Among Insular Pacific societies, pigs are the most important livestock. In North and South America, the majority of societies have no animal husbandry at all, although 24% of North American societies herd horses, and 11% of South American societies tend pigs. Note that sources on Indian societies deal with the postcontact period, mostly referring to the nineteenth century.

Gathering, hunting, and fishing, as important subsistence activities, are each more prevalent in North America than elsewhere. When gathering, hunting, and fishing are combined, we find many societies in several ethnographic areas depending heavily or moderately heavily upon this combination. Almost 90% of all North American societies fall into this category; also, 70% of South American societies, 30% of Insular Pacific societies, and 16% of East Eurasian societies.

Sex division of labor in the subsistence economy indicates roughly the relative contribution made by men and women to the supply of animal and vegetable products for food and raw materials. It indicates only to a limited extent the assignment of tasks according to sex, for even where men and women participate equally in a given subsistence activity, such as fishing or agriculture, the specific tools and techniques employed are likely to differ significantly. Thus, in speaking of the Siamese Tai, Hanks and Hanks (1964: 200) say: "Both sexes fish, but the throw of the net and spear are for males." These qualitative differences in the manner of participation in a given subsistence activity are not revealed by the codes nor by the totals, which provide only a quantitative indication of the significance of the participation of the sexes in the subsistence activities.

In the following discussion, our totals refer to those societies in which the activity in question is present and not unimportant. Since, as noted, the importance of the subsistence activities varies from region to region, this fact should be kept in mind in considering the following figures. Hunting, wherever it exists, is always predominantly a male activity. Where gathering is done, it is predominantly, but not exclusively, a female activity. In some societies (8% of the total) men do predominate in this activity and in some others (14%) it is an equally shared pursuit. The region with greatest male participation in gathering is the Insular Pacific, where in 30% of the societies it is primarily a male activity and in another 30% it is a shared activity. In all other regions, women predominate in gathering in the vast majority of societies.

Fishing, on the other hand, is primarily a male activity in all areas of the world. On a worldwide basis, women predominate in fishing in only 6% of the societies, and in only one region, Africa, do we find fishing to be women's work in as many as 15% of the societies. Equal participation in fishing is greatest in the Insular

Pacific area, where it is, however, found in only 27% of all societies. East Eurasia follows, with equal participation of the sexes in 21% of all societies.

Animal husbandry is another activity largely performed by men. Here again, the Insular Pacific region is a notable exception. In this area, women predominate in animal husbandry in 55% of societies, while men predominate in only 27% of all societies. It is important to note here that caring for large animals is rare in the Insular Pacific region, where the most common type of animal husbandry is the tending of pigs. This contrasts sharply with other regions of the world, where cattle raising or the tending of equine animals is most common. South America is also atypical. In this region, in over 50% of all societies, either animals are cared for largely by women or the activity is shared by men and women. Animal husbandry is, however, relatively rare in South American societies for which information is available.

Agriculture differs from the other subsistence activities in that each geographical region seems to have its own characteristic pattern of division of labor between the sexes. In Africa, women predominate in agriculture in more than 50% of all societies. Women also predominate in agricultural work in 43% of South American societies. In both of these areas, men and women carry on an equal share of the agricultural work in more than 25% of the societies. This division of labor may well be related to the existence of a large percentage of societies with shifting agriculture (71% in Africa and 70% in South America) and, although this is not shown by our figures, to the importance of tropical root crops in these areas. In the Circum-Mediterranean area, men predominate in agricultural work in almost 70% of the societies. East Eurasian societies tend toward equal participation of the sexes (53% of all societies). In these two regions we find the largest number of societies with intensive agriculture: 78% of the societies in the Circum-Mediterranean and 50% in East Eurasia. In the Insular Pacific area, in the 111 societies for which we have data on the relative participation of the sexes in agriculture, in 24% agriculture is men's work, in 34% it is women's work, and in 41% the activity is shared. This is the highest percentage of equal participation in agriculture in any of the regions. In this area, horticulture is practiced by 63% of the societies. Agriculture is relatively unimportant in North America. Where agriculture does exist, women predominate in 42% of the societies and men predominate in another 42%. There is equal participation in agriculture in only 16% of the societies, the lowest percentage of any of the regions.

This lack of consistency in sex division of labor in agriculture among the six geographical regions is of importance. On the one hand it seems to be influenced, as noted, by variations in the predominance of different types of agriculture among the regions. This variation in turn reflects ecological and technological differences among the regions with respect to climates and soils and types of crops, as well as tools and techniques of cultivation. However, other factors appear to influence the division of labor as well. If we compare the two areas with shifting agriculture, where women, as we have seen, predominate in agricultural work in roughly similar proportions, Table 5 shows that there is a much heavier dependence on agriculture in sub-Saharan Africa than in South America and that there is also a much larger percentage of societies with intensive agriculture in Africa. It is interesting to note that in the total column of Table 14, where the worldwide figures on sex division of labor in agriculture are given, we find an almost equal distribution of societies in each of the categories: equal participation, predominance of women, and predominance of men. However, from the total figures alone we could not predict the wide variations among the separate areas, nor the lack of consistency, such that no two areas quite agree in the distribution of societies according to sex division of labor in agriculture.

This is in sharp contrast to the sex division of labor in other subsistence activities (Tables 10-13). These tables show clear similarities among several—or in some cases all—world regions.

The preceding discussion suggests that with the possible exception of agriculture, there exists some degree of polarization among the sexes, with a given activity in a given area being assigned primarily either to men or to women. The geographic area in which equal participation is greatest is East Eurasia, followed closely by the Insular Pacific. The activity in which equal participation is greatest is agriculture.

Table 15 reports on the presence or absence of the several subsistence activities as they are distributed among the societies for which data on sex division of labor are available. Unfortunately, this is a much smaller number of societies than those for which dependence on particular subsistence activities is shown (Tables 1-7). The completeness of coverage varies both by subject and by area. The fullest coverage is available for agriculture, the least information for gathering. Most complete information is available for hunting in North America. In spite of this limitation, a number of interesting observations emerge. Thus while societies may lack one or more subsistence activity, few societies depend exclusively on one activity. Even agricultural societies with or without animal husbandry will generally supplement their diets and their supply of raw materials by some small-scale activity of gathering, hunting, and/or fishing. Table 15, therefore, does not include any overall totals, but only the totals for each activity. Each activity and each world area have their own distribution. Thus, while hunting is the activity most likely to be present (only 9% of 816 societies lack this activity), animal husbandry is most likely to be absent (it is present in only 62% of 413 societies), and, as we already know, it is rarest in the Americas. The area with the lowest incidence of gathering (33% present) and fishing (49% present) is the Circum-Mediterranean, yet hunting is present in 81% of its 84 societies. The area with the least incidence of agriculture is North America (only 32% present). Yet in South America, where 88% of 827 societies practice agriculture, the incidence of societies involved in gathering, hunting, and fishing ranges between 95 and 100%. While in North America a combination of hunting, gathering, and fishing appears to be primary, in the Insular Pacific it is fishing and agriculture that have the largest percentages.

Craft specialization (Table 16) is found among only 41% of all societies (371 out of 863). It is important to realize that specialization here means restriction of the activity to a small skilled group. Crafts performed by a variety of persons throughout a society are not included in this count. In the Circum-Mediterranean area, 86% of all societies have craft specialization. Among both African and East Eurasian societies, 71% have some craft specialization. One-third of Insular Pacific societies fall into this category. On the other hand, in North America and South America, only 3% of all societies have any specialized crafts.

Of the 863 societies, only 14 have any industrial specialization (Table 17), and 13 of these are in the Circum-Mediterranean area: Neapolitans, Greeks (village of Vasilika), Spaniards (Andalusia), Brazilians (village of Cruz das Almas, near São Paulo), French Canadians (Parish of St. Denis), New Englanders (central Connecticut), Dutch (Anlo Parish in Drente province), Lithuanians, Ukranians, Czechs (Hana District of central Moravia), Byelorussians, Syrians (village of Tell Toqaan), and Lebanese (village of Munsif). The remaining society in this group is Japan in the East Eurasian area.

Social Structure, Political Organization, and Religion (Tables 18-24)

Tables 18-24, which are presented in this section, deal with several subjects. Under the heading of Social Structure we consider settlement pattern (Table 18), stratification (Table 19) and presence or absence of slavery (Table 20). The next group of tables deals with the local community. First we consider the office of local headman, indicating both the distribution of that office as well as the method of succession to it (Table 21). We next proceed to data on the distribution of a jurisdictional hierarchy beyond the local level (Table 22) and of the mean size of the local community (Table 23). Table 24 concerns belief in high gods, both its distribution and the type of belief involved.

Among the various settlement patterns, the compact or complex type is found most frequently. More than 50% of all societies in Africa, the Circum-Mediterranean, East Eurasia, Insular Pacific, and South America are settled in this way. Scattered neighborhoods represent a second important settlement pattern in Africa and to a lesser extent in Insular Pacific and Circum-Mediterranean societies. Seminomadic groups account for 67% of the North American societies and about 20% of East Eurasian and South American societies. Migratory bands are characteristic of a small number of societies. African and Insular Pacific areas have the lowest proportion of migratory bands and seminomadic groups. Compact, but impermanent, settlements are very rare.

Table 18: Settlement Pattern
(Column 28)

Code	Type of Settlement	Total		Sub-Saharan Africa		Circum-Mediterranean		East Eurasia		Insular Pacific		North America		South America	
		No.	%	No.	%	No.	%	No.	%	No.	%	No.	%	No.	%
	Total	**863**	**100**	**238**	**100**	**96**	**100**	**94**	**100**	**127**	**100**	**219**	**100**	**89**	**100**
1	Migratory bands	61	7	8	3	10	10	6	6	10	8	16	7	11	12
2	Scattered neighborhoods	176	20	91	38	22	23	12	13	34	27	7	3	10	11
3	Seminomadic or semisedentary communities	208	24	11	5	11	12	19	20	3	2	147	67	17	19
4	Compact, permanent towns or villages; or complex towns with outlying settlements	405	47	124	52	53	55	52	55	79	62	49	22	48	54
5	Compact, impermanent villages shifting locations every few years	13	2	4	2	-	-	5	5	1	1	-	-	3	3

Table 19: Stratification of Freemen
(Column 29)

Code	Type of Stratification	Total		Sub-Saharan Africa		Circum-Mediterranean		East Eurasia		Insular Pacific		North America		South America	
		No.	%	No.	%	No.	%	No.	%	No.	%	No.	%	No.	%.
	Total	**774**	**100**	**204**	**100**	**82**	**100**	**77**	**100**	**124**	**100**	**205**	**100**	**82**	**100**
1,2	No class distinctions	369	48	96	47	14	17	18	23	55	44	123	60	63	77
3,4	Socially important wealth distinctions, but no hereditary social classes	156	20	28	14	13	16	23	30	27	22	56	27	9	11
5,6	Two distinct social classes, with the upper class influencing distribution of scarce resources	189	24	73	36	26	32	19	25	39	32	25	12	7	8
7,8	Complex social classes and extensive occupational differentation	60	8	7	3	29	35	17	22	3	2	1	1	3	4

Table 20: Slavery
(Column 29)

Code	Incidence of Slavery	Total		Sub-Saharan Africa		Circum-Mediterranean		East Eurasia		Insular Pacific		North America		South America	
		No.	%	No.	%	No.	%	No.	%	No.	%	No.	%	No.	%
	Total	**774**	**100**	**204**	**100**	**82**	**100**	**77**	**100**	**124**	**100**	**205**	**100**	**82**	**100**
1,3,5,7	No slavery	411	53	44	22	32	39	34	44	98	79	143	70	60	73
2,4,6,8	Slavery present at time of observation or abolished shortly before that time	363	47	160	78	50	61	43	56	26	21	62	30	22	27

Table 21: Method of Succession to Office of Local Headman
(Column 30)

Code	Type of Succession	Total		Sub-Saharan Africa		Circum-Mediterranean		East Eurasia		Insular Pacific		North America		South America	
		No.	%	No.	%	No.	%	No.	%	No.	%	No.	%	No.	%
	Total	**700**	**100**	**193**	**100**	**63**	**100**	**73**	**100**	**111**	**100**	**199**	**100**	**61**	**100**
	Nonhereditary														
1	By appointment, influence, or seniority	82	12	21	11	9	14	12	16	13	12	23	12	4	7
2	By election or consensus	154	22	18	9	21	33	21	29	18	16	60	30	16	26
	Hereditary														
3	Matrilineal heir	74	11	32	17	3	5	4	5	12	11	16	8	7	11
4	Patrilineal heir	306	44	103	53	18	29	29	40	48	43	79	40	29	48
5	Absence of office	84	12	19	10	12	19	7	10	20	18	21	11	5	8

Table 22: Jurisdictional Hierarchy Beyond the Local Level
(Column 31)

Code	Number of Levels Beyond Local Level	Total		Sub-Saharan Africa		Circum-Mediterranean		East Eurasia		Insular Pacific		North America		South America	
		No.	%	No.	%	No.	%	No.	%	No.	%	No.	%	No.	%
	Total	**841**	**100**	**237**	**100**	**84**	**100**	**91**	**100**	**126**	**100**	**217**	**100**	**86**	**100**
1,5	None	396	47	60	25	9	11	28	31	71	56	158	73	70	81
2,6	One	256	30	102	43	23	27	29	32	38	30	52	24	12	14
3,7	Two	110	13	54	23	18	21	14	15	14	11	7	3	3	4
4,8	Three or four	79	9	21	9	34	41	20	22	3	2	-	-	1	1

Table 23: Mean Size of the Local Community
(Column 32)

Code	Average Population	Total		Sub-Saharan Africa		Circum-Mediterranean		East Eurasia		Insular Pacific		North America		South America	
		No.	%	No.	%	No.	%	No.	%	No.	%	No.	%	No.	%
	Total	**465**	**100**	**100**	**100**	**48**	**100**	**72**	**100**	**65**	**100**	**125**	**100**	**55**	**100**
1	Less than 50	91	20	6	6	2	4	11	15	10	15	38	30	24	44
2	50 to 199	172	37	38	38	7	15	27	38	29	45	50	40	21	38
3	200 to 1,000	115	25	41	41	4	8	13	18	22	34	30	24	5	9
4	Over 1,000	87	19	15	15	35	73	21	29	4	6	7	6	5	9

Table 24: Belief in High Gods
(Column 33)

Code	Type of High God Belief	Total No. %	Sub-Saharan Africa No. %	Circum-Mediterranean No. %	East Eurasia No. %	Insular Pacific No. %	North America No. %	South America No. %
	Total	**596 100**	**147 100**	**81 100**	**71 100**	**77 100**	**153 100**	**67 100**
1	Belief exists, but high god is not concerned with human affairs.	195 33	96 65	8 10	12 17	13 17	41 27	25 37
2	Belief exists; high god is concerned with human affairs, but not with morality.	40 7	18 12	1 1	10 14	- -	7 5	4 6
3	Belief exists; high god is concerned with human affairs and with morality.	124 21	12 8	70 86	13 18	6 8	13 8	10 15
4	Belief in high god is absent or not reported in the literature and assumed absent.	237 40	21 14	2 3	36 51	58 75	92 60	28 42

Stratification among freemen tends to be relatively simple. No stratification at all among freemen exists in 47% of African societies, 60% of North American societies, and 77% of South American societies. The incidence of wealth distinction without social classes ranges from 11% in South America to 30% in East Eurasia. A stratification system of two distinct classes exists in about one-third of the societies of Africa, the Circum-Mediterranean region, and Insular Pacific groups. The only areas having an appreciable amount of complex stratification are the Circum-Mediterranean (35%) and East Eurasia (22%).

Slavery is predominant in Africa, being present* in almost 80% of these societies. In the Circum-Mediterranean area, slavery exists in 61% of the societies. Over 50% of East Eurasian groups have slavery as well. By contrast, in the other regions, slavery is present in only 20% to 30% of the societies.

The hereditary succession to the office of local headman is most important among African societies (70%). In other areas of the world, hereditary succession exists in 34% to 59% of the societies. In Insular Pacific and in North and South American societies, hereditary succession is more prevalent than nonhereditary succession. On the other hand, in the Circum-Mediterranean area, nonhereditary succession is proportionately more prevalent. In East Eurasia, the number of societies with hereditary and non-hereditary succession is the same. Nonhereditary succession is least important in Africa. In many of the world regions where there is hereditary succession to the office of local headman, societies in which the patrilineal heir succeeds are much more numerous than those in which the position goes to an heir in the matriline.

The presence of jurisdictional levels beyond the local level may be considered an indication of political complexity. The vast majority of societies in all areas, except the Circum-Mediter-ranean, have a relatively simple political jurisdictional structure. More than 60% of these societies have either one level beyond the local level or no levels beyond the local level. The Circum-Medi-terranean area is the exception, with more than 60% of its socie-

---

*It should be noted that the ethnographic present is used here. "Slavery present," therefore, means the time period at which the societies in question are described. It also includes societies where slavery was officially abolished close to the time of ethnographic study.

ties having two, three, or four levels beyond the local level, hence the greatest political complexity. In Africa and East Eurasia, more than 30% of the societies have two, three, or four levels. By comparison, the Insular Pacific and North and South American societies have much less political complexity.

In most regions, the mean size of the local community tends to be between fifty and one thousand people. Among the Circum-Mediterranean groups, however, 73% of the societies have local communities of over one thousand average. On the other hand, in South America 44% of the societies have an average local population of less than fifty.

Belief in a high god is present in the majority of societies of Africa, the Circum-Mediterranean area, and South America. In the Insular Pacific and North American areas, the majority of societies do not have such a belief. About one-half of the societies of East Eurasia have a belief in a high god. Where a belief in a high god exists, such belief is generally not connected with morality, except in the Circum-Mediterranean area. In this area, 88% of the societies have a belief in a high god concerned with the moral affairs of human beings.

Marriage and Kinship (Tables 25-32)

The next group of tables deals with various aspects of marriage and kinship. Tables 25 and 26 are both based on Column 34. By community organization, we mean in this context whether or not communities are segmented or not, whether there are component parts, and what rules if any control marriage within these component units and in the community as a whole. Table 27 shows the distribution of marriage forms, and Table 28 that of family forms. These are followed by two tables (29-30) dealing with marital residence and kin groups respectively. The concluding tables in this section (Tables 31-32) deal with mode of marriage and cousin marriage in terms of laterality. The data on marriage and family are among the most complete in the *Atlas*.

Code	Type of Community	Total		Sub-Saharan Africa		Circum-Mediterranean		East Eurasia		Insular Pacific		North America		South America	
		No.	%	No.	%	No.	%	No.	%	No.	%	No.	%	No.	%
	Total	**793**	**100**	**222**	**100**	**76**	**100**	**92**	**100**	**121**	**100**	**203**	**100**	**79**	**100**
1	Nonsegmented Agamous	288	36	47	21	33	43	40	44	32	27	107	53	29	37
2	Clan (exogamous)	153	19	83	37	12	16	13	14	21	17	19	9	5	6
3	Demes (endogamous)	69	9	-	-	13	17	9	10	6	5	20	10	21	27
4	Exogamous, no clan	94	12	17	8	7	9	11	12	6	5	40	20	13	16
5	Segmented Nonexogamous	182	23	73	33	11	15	16	17	55	46	17	8	10	13
6	Exogamous	7	1	2	1	-	-	3	3	1	1	-	-	1	1

Table 26: Community Organization (Marriage Rules)
(Column 34)

Code	Marriage Rules	Total		Sub-Saharan Africa		Circum-Mediterranean		East Eurasia		Insular Pacific		North America		South America	
		No.	%	No.	%	No.	%	No.	%	No.	%	No.	%	No.	%
	Total	**793**	**100**	**222**	**100**	**76**	**100**	**92**	**100**	**121**	**100**	**203**	**100**	**79**	**100**
1	Agamous	288	36	47	21	33	43	40	44	32	27	107	53	29	37
2,4,6	Exogamous	254	32	102	46	19	25	27	29	28	23	59	29	19	23
3	Endogamous	69	9	-	-	13	17	9	10	6	5	20	10	21	27
5	Nonexogamous, no other rule specified	182	23	73	33	11	15	16	17	55	46	17	8	10	13

Table 27: Marriage Form
(Columns 35-38)

Code	Marriage Form	Total		Sub-Saharan Africa		Circum-Mediterranean		East Eurasia		Insular Pacific		North America		South America	
		No.	%	No.	%	No.	%	No.	%	No.	%	No.	%	No.	%
	Total	**854**	**100**	**238**	**100**	**95**	**100**	**93**	**100**	**124**	**100**	**216**	**100**	**88**	**100**
1	Monogamy	137	16	2	1	36	38	20	22	30	24	31	14	18	21
2	Monogamy, with occasional polygyny	334	39	34	14	25	26	58	62	64	52	106	49	47	53
3	Polyandry	4	-	-	-	-	-	3	3	1	1	-	-	-	-
4	Polygyny	379	44	202	85	34	36	12	13	29	23	79	37	23	26

Table 28: Family Form
(Columns 35-38)

All Codes in Columns	Type of Family	Total		Sub-Saharan Africa		Circum-Mediterranean		East Eurasia		Insular Pacific		North America		South America	
		No.	%	No.	%	No.	%	No.	%	No.	%	No.	%	No.	%
	Total	**856**	**100**	**238**	**100**	**96**	**100**	**93**	**100**	**125**	**100**	**216**	**100**	**88**	**100**
35	Independent	427	50	132	56	50	52	37	40	72	58	91	42	45	51
36	Large extended	149	17	53	22	12	13	11	12	19	15	34	16	20	23
37	Small extended	241	28	50	21	27	28	32	34	28	22	83	38	21	24
38	Stem	39	5	3	1	7	7	13	14	6	5	8	4	2	2

Table 29: Marital Residence
(Column 39)

Code	Residence Rule	Total No.	Total %	Sub-Saharan Africa No.	Sub-Saharan Africa %	Circum-Mediterranean No.	Circum-Mediterranean %	East Eurasia No.	East Eurasia %	Insular Pacific No.	Insular Pacific %	North America No.	North America %	South America No.	South America %
	Total	**859**	**100**	**237**	**100**	**96**	**100**	**94**	**100**	**126**	**100**	**218**	**100**	**88**	**100**
1	Nonestablishment of a common household	8	1	1	-	1	1	1	1	5	4	-	-	-	-
2	Neolocal	40	5	5	2	12	13	2	2	2	2	11	5	8	9
3	Patrilocal	391	46	178	75	59	61	65	69	47	37	30	14	12	14
4	Virilocal	198	23	17	7	18	19	12	13	32	25	95	44	24	27
5	Matrilocal	43	5	4	2	-	-	6	6	10	8	18	8	5	6
6	Uxorilocal	69	8	-	-	-	-	5	5	8	6	28	13	28	32
7	Avunculocal	37	4	23	10	2	2	-	-	4	3	6	3	2	2
8	Optional—Ambilocal	73	8	9	4	4	4	3	3	18	14	30	14	9	10

Table 30: Kin Groups
(Column 40)

Code	Kin Groups	Total		Sub-Saharan Africa		Circum-Mediterranean		East Eurasia		Insular Pacific		North America		South America	
		No.	%	No.	%	No.	%	No.	%	No.	%	No.	%	No.	%
	Total	**860**	**100**	**238**	**100**	**96**	**100**	**94**	**100**	**126**	**100**	**219**	**100**	**87**	**100**
1	Patrilineal	396	46	173	73	57	59	66	70	43	34	42	19	15	17
2	Matrilineal	120	14	36	15	7	7	8	9	28	22	34	16	7	8
3	Double descent	34	4	17	7	2	2	3	3	12	10	-	-	-	-
4	Cognatic	310	36	12	5	30	31	17	18	43	34	143	65	65	75

Table 31: Mode of Marriage
(Column 41)

Code	Marriage Modes	Total		Sub-Saharan Africa		Circum-Mediterranean		East Eurasia		Insular Pacific		North America		South America	
		No.	%	No.	%	No.	%	No.	%	No.	%	No.	%	No.	%
	Total	**860**	**100**	**238**	**100**	**96**	**100**	**94**	**100**	**127**	**100**	**218**	**100**	**87**	**100**
1	Bride-price or bride service	502	58	214	90	66	69	58	62	53	42	68	31	43	49
2	Dowry	23	3	-	-	13	13	8	8	2	2	-	-	-	-
3	Exchange of gifts or of persons	82	10	11	5	3	3	2	2	35	28	28	13	3	4
4	Token bride-price or absence of marriage mode	253	29	13	5	14	15	26	28	37	29	122	56	41	47

Table 32: Cousin Marriage
(Column 42)

Code	Rules of Cousin Marriage	Total		Sub-Saharan Africa		Circum-Mediterranean		East Eurasia		Insular Pacific		North America		South America	
		No.	%	No.	%	No.	%	No.	%	No.	%	No.	%	No.	%
	Total	**762**	**100**	**204**	**100**	**73**	**100**	**87**	**100**	**123**	**100**	**202**	**100**	**73**	**100**
1	Nonlateral	474	62	134	66	30	41	30	34	86	70	167	83	27	37
2	Duolateral	155	20	46	23	6	8	27	31	20	16	24	12	32	44
3	Quadrilateral	78	10	9	4	34	47	14	16	8	6	5	2	8	11
4	Matrilateral	32	4	6	3	-	-	11	13	8	7	4	2	3	4
5	Trilateral	19	2	7	3	3	4	5	6	1	1	1	-	2	3
6	Patrilateral	4	1	2	1	-	-	-	-	-	-	1	-	1	1
7	Unilateral	-	-	-	-	-	-	-	-	-	-	-	-	-	-

Monogamy is characteristic of only 16% of the world societies, while plural marriage is permitted in the vast majority of societies in all areas of the world. In Africa, 85% of the societies are polygynous, and another 14% practice monogamy with occasional polygyny, making a total of 99% of societies where polygyny may be practiced and does occur in at least some instances. Although Circum-Mediterranean societies have a fair amount of polygyny, this area has the highest proportion of societies imposing monogamy (38%). In East Eurasia, 62% of the societies are monogamous with occasional polygyny. Also, about one-half of the societies of the Insular Pacific and North and South America tend to be monogamous, with occasional polygyny. Polyandry is a very rare form of marriage, present in only four societies in this tabulation.

The independent family is the accepted family form in one-half of all the societies tabulated. This proportion holds generally in all areas, except for East Eurasia, where the incidence of the independent family drops to 40%, and North America, where the proportion is 42%. Societies characterized by the small extended family represent 38% of the North American and 34% of the East Eurasian groups. Africa and South America have the largest proportion of societies with the large extended family, but even in these areas it exists in less than 25% of the societies. The stem family is rare.

Patrilineal kin groups predominate in the African, East Eurasian, and Circum-Mediterranean areas. By contrast, in North and South America, 65% and 75% of the societies, respectively, have cognatic kin groups. In the Insular Pacific area, patrilineal, matrilineal, and cognatic kin groups seem to be rather evenly distributed. Matrilineal kin groups do not predominate in any area, and kin groups based on double descent are relatively rare in all areas and totally absent in North and South America.

We may consider community organization as presented here from two points of view: with respect to marriage rules and with respect to internal segmentation. As far as marriage rules are concerned, slightly more than one-third of the world societies coded live in agamous groups. This varies from a high of 53% in North America to a low of 21% in Africa. The Circum-Mediterranean area and East Eurasia also are above average on agamous organization. Somewhat less than one-third of the world societies coded are seen to be exogamous, with the highest percentage (46%) in Africa. Endogamous organizations, however, are relatively rare, and are represented by only 9% of the societies. Endogamous organizations are not recorded for Africa at all, but reach their highest percentage (27%) in South America, where, in fact, they exceed exogamous organizations in frequency. The remaining groups are nonexogamous, with no specific marriage rules stated. These range from a high of 46% in the Insular Pacific to a low of 8% in North America.

With respect to our second point, we find a variety of organizations and marriage rules represented in nonsegmented communities. Demes, clans, exogamy without clans, and agamous communities all belong under this heading, and together they account for three-quarters of the societies coded. Segmented communities account for the remaining quarter. These are mostly nonexogamous societies, for which no rules are specified. This latter type accounts, however, for almost one-half of the societies in the Insular Pacific and one-third of the African societies. Elsewhere, segmented societies are rare, and segmented exogamous societies are totally unrecorded for the Circum-Mediterranean area and for North America.

Marital residence throughout the world is most likely to be patrilocal (46% of all societies), but this is true primarily for Africa (75%), East Eurasia (69%), and the Circum-Mediterranean area (61%). It is least likely in South America, where patrilocal residence characterizes only 14% of the societies. Second in importance in a worldwide comparison is virilocal residence, which reaches its highest incidence (44%) in North America, followed by South America (27%) and the Insular Pacific (25%). It is rare only in Africa (7%). Next in rank is uxorilocal residence, with 32% in South America and 13% in North America. Thus virilocal and uxorilocal residence in the Americas contrast interestingly with an emphasis on patrilocal residence in the Old World. Optional ambilocal residence is most frequent in North America and the Insular Pacific (14% each). Surprisingly, matrilocal and avunculocal residence are as rare as neolocal residence, the latter being found most typically in the Circum-Mediterranean area (13%).

Cousin marriage of the nonlateral type is generally most frequent and reaches its highest proportion (83%) in North America, the Insular Pacific (70%), and Africa (66%). Duolateral cousin marriage is most characteristic of South America (44%), and the quadrilateral type is most likely in the Circum-Mediterranean area (47%). All other forms are rare, with unilateral nonreported and patrilateral occurring only 4 times in 762 societies. The much discussed matrilateral type of cousin marriage is represented by a total of 32 cases, 11 of which are reported from East Eurasia and 8 from the Insular Pacific.

The bride-price or bride service are the most widely used marriage modes in Africa (90%), the Circum-Mediterranean (69%), East Eurasia (62%), and South America (49%). In North America, a token bride-price or no marriage mode is used in 56% of the societies. Gift exchange or exchange of persons is found rarely, except in Insular Pacific societies, where almost 30% use this mode. The dowry is nonexistent except for a very few societies in the Circum-Mediterranean, East Eurasian, and Insular Pacific areas.

Social Restrictions and Games (Tables 33-37)

The final group of five tables deals with social controls of sex life and adolescence and with games. Tables 33 and 34, on norms of premarital sex behavior and on the postpartum sex taboo, have data on only a small number of societies, as does Table 37, dealing with the distribution of several types of games. Table 35, Segregation of Adolescent Boys, covers about two-thirds of the *Atlas* societies, while Table 36, Male Genital Mutilation, has data for over 800 societies.

Little restriction is put on premarital sex relations in most areas of the world. More than two-thirds of the societies in all areas except the Circum-Mediterranean provide few restrictions on this activity. In the Circum-Mediterranean area, however, 59% of all societies are concerned with virginity and early marriage of females.

Duration of postpartum sex taboos varies widely. In Africa, 67% of the societies impose a taboo of more than one year. In East Eurasia, on the other hand, in 44% of the societies the taboo is for less than one month. Of the societies in the Circum-Mediterranean, Insular Pacific, and North and South American areas, 40% or more impose taboos of between one month and one year.

Table 33: Norms of Premarital Sex Behavior
(Column 43)

Code	Type of Norms	Total		Sub-Saharan Africa		Circum-Mediterranean		East Eurasia		Insular Pacific		North America		South America	
		No.	%	No.	%	No.	%	No.	%	No.	%	No.	%	No.	%
	Total	**456**	**100**	**93**	**100**	**51**	**100**	**63**	**100**	**75**	**100**	**126**	**100**	**48**	**100**
1	Little restriction	307	67	65	70	21	41	42	67	56	75	89	71	34	71
2	Early marriage of females, or insistence on virginity	149	33	28	30	30	59	21	33	19	25	37	29	14	29

Table 34: Postpartum Sex Taboo
(Column 44)

Code	Length of Taboo Period	Total		Sub-Saharan Africa		Circum-Mediterranean		East Eurasia		Insular Pacific		North America		South America	
		No.	%	No.	%	No.	%	No.	%	No.	%	No.	%	No.	%
	Total	**304**	**100**	**72**	**100**	**14**	**100**	**25**	**100**	**47**	**100**	**109**	**100**	**37**	**100**
1	Less than one month	58*	19	4	6	3	21	11	44	8	17	24	22	8	22
2	One month to one year	132	43	20	28	6	43	9	36	19	40	59	54	19	51
3	Over one year	114	38	48	67	5	36	5	20	20	43	26	24	10	27

*Included in this number are two societies with no taboo at all, the Neapolitans and the Lepcha.

Table 35: Segregation of Adolescent Boys
(Column 45)

Code	Degree of Segregation	Total		Sub-Saharan Africa		Circum-Mediterranean		East Eurasia		Insular Pacific		North America		South America	
		No.	%	No.	%	No.	%	No.	%	No.	%	No.	%	No.	%
	Total	**611**	**100**	**143**	**100**	**56**	**100**	**84**	**100**	**98**	**100**	**171**	**100**	**59**	**100**
1	Absence of segregation	370	61	31	22	44	79	65	77	36	37	150	88	44	75
2	Partial segregation	101	16	60	42	9	16	2	2	12	12	14	8	4	7
3	Complete segregation	140	23	52	36	3	5	17	20	50	51	7	4	11	19

Table 36: Male Genital Mutilation
(Column 46)

Code	Age at Which Mutilation Occurs	Total No.	Total %	Sub-Saharan Africa No.	Sub-Saharan Africa %	Circum-Mediterranean No.	Circum-Mediterranean %	East Eurasia No.	East Eurasia %	Insular Pacific No.	Insular Pacific %	North America No.	North America %	South America No.	South America %
	Total	**815**	**100**	**216**	**100**	**89**	**100**	**92**	**100**	**110**	**100**	**219**	**100**	**89**	**100**
1	No mutilation occurs	587	72	96	44	25	28	76	83	82	74	219	100	89	100
2	Ten years and younger	88	11	38	18	35	39	8	9	7	6	-	-	-	-
3	Eleven to fifteen years	78	10	55	25	8	9	2	2	13	12	-	-	-	-
4	Sixteen years and over	15	2	8	4	5	6	-	-	2	2	-	-	-	-
5	Age not specified in the literature	47	6	19	9	16	18	6	6	6	6	-	-	-	-

Table 37: Types of Games
(Column 47)

Code	Nature of Games	Total		Sub-Saharan Africa		Circum-Mediterranean		East Eurasia		Insular Pacific		North America		South America	
		No.	%	No.	%	No.	%	No.	%	No.	%	No.	%	No.	%
	Total	**391**	**100**	**41**	**100**	**24**	**100**	**40**	**100**	**47**	**100**	**189**	**100**	**50**	**100**
1	Physical skill	97	25	7	17	3	12	16	40	34	72	8	4	29	58
2	Physical skill and chance	197	50	2	5	-	-	4	10	7	15	176	93	8	16
3	Physical skill and strategy	21	5	15	37	1	4	4	10	1	2	-	-	-	-
4	Skill, chance, and strategy	45	12	14	34	16	67	10	25	1	2	3	2	1	2
5	All others	31	8	3	7	4	17	6	15	4	9	2	1	12	24

It should be kept in mind that data on this subject are scarce, and that the large number of societies with no information makes these statistics less reliable than others. (Out of a possible 863 societies, data are available for only 304.)

Segregation of adolescent boys is widespread in Africa and to a lesser extent in Insular Pacific societies. In all other areas, however, over 70% of the societies do not segregate adolescent boys.

Male genital mutilation is most prevalent in the Circum-Mediterranean area (72% of all societies). In Africa, such mutilations occur in 56% of the societies. In all other areas, very few societies have such practices.

Relatively little information is available on games. The best data exist for North America, where in 93% of the societies games combining physical skill and chance predominate. From the sparse information for other areas, it seems that outside of North America, games of chance are not as important as games of physical skill and strategy.

Some Further Comparisons

In the preceding section we have presented data on various aspects of social organization in the form of a series of tables, together with some comments and interpretations. Here we wish to re-examine some of these data by regrouping them somewhat and presenting them in the visual form of charts.

Although we argue generally in opposition to polarization of data and the use of two-by-two tables for correlational studies, for the purposes of these charts we have, in fact, condensed the more refined and complex data of some of the tables into twofold divisions. We do this in part to contrast the kinds of results obtained by these two types of groupings and in part to highlight certain facets of our data.

Chart I presents some of the data on subsistence economy. As such, it should be compared with Tables 5-7. In Chart IA, we contrast heavy dependence on agriculture (46-100%) with little dependence (0-45%). In inspecting this chart, it becomes immediately apparent that the Americas are in sharp contrast to the rest of the world with respect to this variable, and, moreover, that the worldwide average of 61% "heavy dependence" is greatly influenced by the low figures for North and South America. Yet, the difference between the Americas is a major one as well.

Chart I
Subsistence Economy

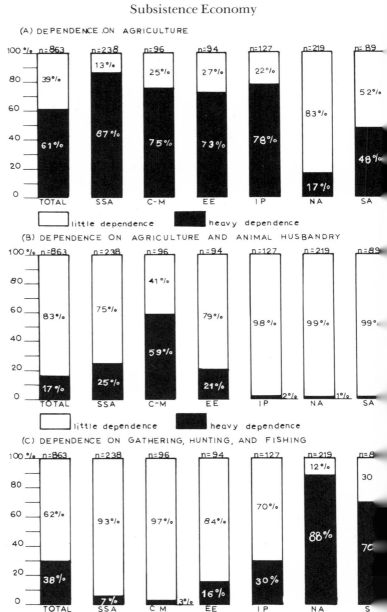

(A) DEPENDENCE ON AGRICULTURE

(B) DEPENDENCE ON AGRICULTURE AND ANIMAL HUSBANDRY

(C) DEPENDENCE ON GATHERING, HUNTING, AND FISHING

Chart II
Sex Division of Labor

(A) SEX DIVISION OF LABOR IN AGRICULTURE

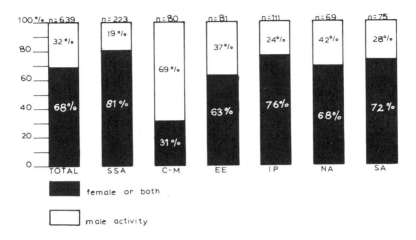

(B)   SEX DIVISION OF LABOR IN ANIMAL HUSBANDRY

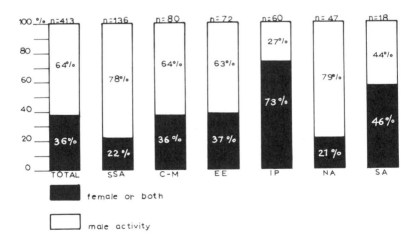

Chart III
Stratification

(A) SLAVERY

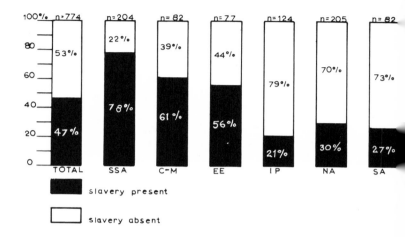

slavery present

slavery absent

(B) STRATIFICATION OF FREEMEN

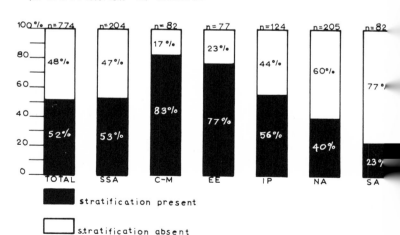

stratification present

stratification absent

Chart IV
Political Organization and Religious Belief

(A) JURISDICTIONAL HIERARCHY ABOVE THE LOCAL LEVEL

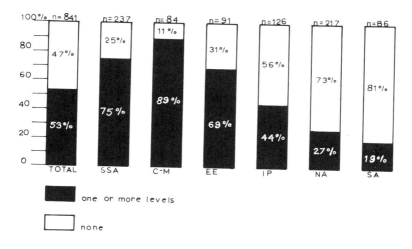

(B) HIGH GOD BELIEF

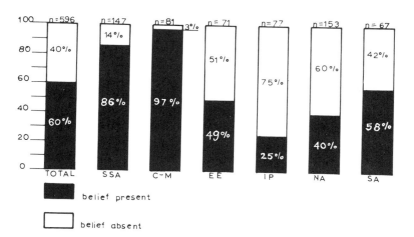

When the combined dependence on agriculture and animal husbandry is considered (Chart IB, Table 7), the Circum-Mediterranean area stands out as the one most dependent on this combination. Together with its neighboring regions, Africa on the one hand and East Eurasia on the other, it stands in sharp contrast to the other three areas, i.e. the Insular Pacific as well as the Americas.

Chart IC presents the data of Table 6 in dichotomized form. Here we have the very opposite picture from that presented by the previous chart. North America leads off with the largest percentage of societies with heavy dependence on a combination of gathering, hunting, and fishing. South America follows behind and is trailed in third place by the Insular Pacific. The three other Old World areas make minimal use of this combination of subsistence activities.

Chart II presents dichotomized data on sex division of labor in two subsistence activities: agriculture (Table 14) and animal husbandry (Table 13). Here we have used only those societies in which the activity is present and not unimportant, as we did in our tables. In contrast to the tables, however, we have here grouped "equal participation of both sexes" with "women perform the activity alone or do appreciably more than men." If one wishes to dichotomize the data, such middle terms must necessarily be assigned to one or the other of the polar terms. In this case, we feel that our assignment helps us to contrast the percentages of societies in each area in which women are involved significantly with a given subsistence activity with those in which they are not. In Chart IIA, Sex Division of Labor in Agriculture, we see that, on a worldwide basis, only about a third of the societies (32%) make agriculture an exclusively male activity. Only in the Circum-Mediterranean area is agriculture a predominantly male activity, with two-thirds of the societies falling into this category. Here, then, the Americas conform generally to the world norm: women participate significantly in agriculture in those societies where this is an important subsistence activity. It is only the Circum-Mediterranean area that strikingly deviates from this norm. It should be noted, however, that these statistics cannot tell us the full contribution of women to subsistence activities in these several regions, since only those societies that do practice agriculture are included here, and in the Americas, these are very much in the minority.

Chart IIB concerns Sex Division of Labor in Animal Husbandry. We have again grouped "equal participation of the sexes" with the category "women perform the activity alone or do appreciably more than men." In spite of this grouping of the data, animal husbandry clearly emerges as a predominantly male activity in about two-thirds of the world societies coded here and in four of the six regions. The greatest exception is presented by the Insular Pacific, where animal husbandry is a predominately male activity in only 27% of the societies and, to a lesser degree, in South America, where this is the case in less than half of the societies (44%).

Chart III presents dichotomized data on two aspects of social structure, Stratification of Freemen and Slavery (Tables 19 and 20). In Chart IIIB we have contrasted all forms of stratification, including differentiations by wealth, with absence of stratification. We find, then, that stratification of some kind is present in a slight majority of all world societies coded (52%) and in four of the six regions. The Americas have least stratification, with South America much less than North America. The overall picture points to a sizable distribution of egalitarian societies, although, as we shall note below, some of the societies that do not make distinctions among freemen do in fact have slavery.

Chart IIIA shows us the distribution of slavery, an institution found to exist in the ethnographic present in 47% of the world societies. With respect to slavery, the world is sharply divided between Africa, the Circum-Mediterranean, and East Eurasia, where slavery predominates (in that order) and the Insular Pacific and the Americas, where it is present in less than a third of the societies.

A comparison of Charts IIIA and IIIB is of some interest. The percentage of societies with stratification of freemen is consistently greater than that with slavery, with the striking exception of Africa, where slavery far exceeds stratification. This is also true in South America, but only to a minimal degree. It would lead one to believe that slavery is present in the other four areas only where there is stratification of freemen as well. This is patently not so, although these data are not arranged here so as to show this.

Chart IV presents data on jurisdictional hierarchy and on belief in high gods by dichotomizing the data of Tables 22 and 24. Chart IVA deals with jurisdictional hierarchy above the local level and contrasts those societies which have no such hierarchy, i.e. for whom the local level is the highest level in a jurisdictional hierarchy. Here again we find, as we have seen several times before, that the Americas fall considerably below the world average, with the Insular Pacific between the Americas and the three great Old World areas. The Circum-Mediterranean is the area with the largest percentage of complex societies, followed by Africa and East Eurasia, in that order.

Chart IVB presents data on belief in high gods. Here we have grouped all such beliefs, whether the deity is conceived of as otiose or active or whether or not we are dealing with ethical monotheism. We have contrasted societies with such beliefs with those for which absence of the belief is reported or the belief is unreported. The reason for this grouping is derived from the research of Swanson (itself derived from Durkheim), relating belief in a high god to societal complexity (numbers of jurisdictional levels). The chart shows a predominance of high god beliefs in the Circum-Mediterranean and Africa. The lowest percentage is found in the Insular Pacific, and East Eurasia places on this score between North and South America. This distribution is somewhat inconsistent with several others that we have discussed, and the reader should again note the variation in totals for the several categories of data presented.

Profiles of World Areas

We now wish to consider briefly the distinctiveness of each major world area as it appears from our tables:

Africa (i.e. sub-Saharan Africa) is distinguished by its great concentration on shifting agriculture, patrilocal residence, patrilineal kin groups, and patrilineal succession to the office of headman. There is extensive polygyny, with 99% of societies coded having one of the two forms of polygyny, and there is high emphasis on marriage by bride-price or bride service, which exist in 90% of the societies. Also, Africa has the highest percentage of societies with emphasis on female participation in agriculture and emphasis on male participation in animal husbandry. It also has the highest percentage of societies having, or having recently had, slavery. It is distinctive for a series of features which have been the subjects of a number of recent cross-cultural studies: the highest percentage of societies showing male genital mutilation at puberty, both partial and complete segregation of adolescent boys, and postpartum sex taboo of one year or more.

The *Circum-Mediterranean* area is distinguished by its great emphasis on intensive agriculture and male participation in agricultural work, large communities, and complex stratification of freemen. Societies in this area more often than elsewhere possess three or four jurisdictional levels above the local level. Belief in a high god concerned with human morality exists in 88% of the societies of this area. There is a highly distinctive emphasis on virginity and early marriage, with dowry used more frequently than elsewhere as a mode of marriage. Where the practice of male genital mutilation exists, it occurs before puberty (ten years or younger).

East Eurasia is second only to the Circum-Mediterranean area in incidence of intensive agriculture, large communities, and complex social classes. The area is also above the world average in the percentage of societies having several jurisdictional levels above the local level. Kin groups are typically patrilineal, with partilocal residence. Mode of marriage is typically by bride-price or service, and there is little restriction on premarital sex. Also, this area has the highest percentage of societies having limited polygyny and stem families, as well as a short period of postpartum sex taboo and absence of segregation of adolescent boys. Male genital mutilation is also generally absent.

The *Insular Pacific* area is distinctive for its high dependence on fishing and horticulture. Settlements are compact and permanent, and communities small. While there is a fair amount of stratification, only 2% of the societies of this area have complex stratification of freemen and only 2% have three or four jurisdictional levels above the local level. The area has the highest percentage of segmented nonexogamous communities. All types of marital residence are represented. Double descent, though rare, is more prevalent here than in the other areas. There is a predominance of monogamy, with occasional polygyny, and of nuclear families. This is also the area with the highest percentage of societies having marriage by exchange. Cousin marriage is mostly nonlateral. This is the area of least restraint on premarital sex, and of the highest percentage of societies having complete segregation of adolescent boys, but there is also a high percentage of societies with an absence of male genital mutilation.

North America is distinctive for its dependence on gathering, hunting, and fishing. A majority of North American societies have a complete lack of agriculture. Settlement patterns are typically seminomadic. This area has the highest percentage of societies with agamous communities, while segmented nonexogamous communities are less frequent than elsewhere. Communities are small, and either the position of local headman is nonhereditary or succession is by the patrilineal heir. Most societies have no stratification of freemen, and even fewer have slavery. Most have no jurisdictional levels above the local level. Marital residence is typically virilocal—rather than patrilocal, as for most other areas. Descent is typically cognatic, and a mode of marriage is absent or occurs only in token form. Marriage mostly takes the form of monogamy, with occasional polygyny, and the family is typically of either the independent nuclear or the stem family form. Segregation of adolescent boys is rare, and male genital mutilation is totally absent.

South America: While almost one-half of societies in this area have a rather high dependence on agriculture, which is mostly of the shifting type, 42% depend on a combination of gathering, hunting, and fishing. Settlement patterns are mostly compact or complex and permanent. There is a higher frequency of endogamous demes than in any other area. Exogamous clans, however, are rare. Local communities are small; indeed, we find here the highest percentage of societies with communities of fifty or less. Most societies have no stratification of freemen, and only 4% have complex stratification. The area has the largest percentage of societies without jurisdictional levels above the local level. Marital residence is distinctive by being most frequently uxorilocal, with the generally preferred patrilocal residence being only a third choice. Kin groups are mostly cognatic; there are no instances of double descent and only a few patrilineal societies. South America has the largest percentage of societies with large extended families, but nonetheless most societies have independent nuclear families. Segregation of adolescent boys is present in only 25% of the societies, and male genital mutilation is totally absent.

Comment

In the preceding section, we have noted the distinctiveness of each region, as shown by our tables. We have found that a characteristic profile emerges for each, as we describe the nature of basic subsistence forms and various aspects of social organization. For example, emphasis on shifting agriculture and high participation of women in agriculture are found independently both in sub-Saharan Africa and in South America. Intensive agriculture is widespread in both the Circum-Mediterranean region and in East Eurasia, where also are found large numbers of societies with complex forms of stratification and two or more levels of jurisdictional hierarchy beyond the local level. These, too, are the areas with the largest mean size of local communities. In other words, the profiles imply likely relationships between subsistence economy and other aspects of culture.

Yet one is struck by the enormous difference between the Americas and the rest of the world. This difference is somewhat moderated for South America by the emphasis on shifting agriculture mentioned above, so that it is primarily North America that is truly distinctive, with its great preponderance of hunting, gathering, and fishing societies. These distinctions are brought more sharply into focus if we contrast North America with the rest of the world with respect to specific economic and societal features. Thus, although heavy dependence on hunting, gathering, and fishing (Table 6) characterizes 77% of North American societies, for the rest of the world this dependence ranges from a high of 28% for South America to none at all in the Circum-Mediterranean region. Conversely, while only 17% of North American societies depend on agriculture for half or more of their subsistence (Table 5), the rest of the world ranges from 48% for South America to 87% for sub-Saharan Africa. Table 8, furthermore, shows us that 66% of North American societies completely lack agriculture, which is true only of from 3% to 13% of the societies in the other regions of the world.

As is to be expected, North American settlement patterns reflect such subsistence activities: 67% of North American societies live in seminomadic or semisedentary communities (Table 18). The highest percentage for this type of settlement pattern in other regions is found in East Eurasia, where it is exhibited by 20% of the societies. Compact permanent towns or villages, fairly common in other areas of the world, are found in only 22% of the North American societies. Yet, perhaps somewhat surprisingly, there is more evidence of stratification to be found in North America than in South America (Table 19); both of these New World regions, however, are far exceeded in the presence of stratification by all the regions of the Old World.

As already noted, more than one-half of North American societies have communities that are nonsegmented and agamous, much in contrast to community forms in the societies of the other regions of the world (Table 25). Almost half of North American societies practice virilocal residence (Table 29), with kin groups typically being cognatic. Virilocal residence is rare elsewhere, as are cognatic kin groups, with the exception of South America (Table 30). Even in respect to types of games, North America is found to be radically deviant, with 93% of the societies having games of physical skill and chance; whereas the range with respect to this type of game in the incidence among societies of the rest of the world varies from 16% in South America to none in the Circum-Mediterranean region (Table 37).

Such great differences between North America and the other regions of the world have also been noted in characteristics not coded in the *Ethnographic Atlas*. For example, in a study of culturally patterned forms of altered states of consciousness, we have found North America to be strikingly different from the rest of the world. We distinguished between two types of altered states: one, termed Possession Trance, is considered to be a manifestation of spirit possession, and the other, termed Trance, is not so interpreted. Of the 120 societies in our North American sample, 92% had Trance, and only 25% had Possession Trance (some societies had both forms). Indeed, a mere 4% had only Possession Trance, and 3% showed no evidence of either type of altered state. South America, with 76% of its societies having Trance and 30% Possession Trance, is the only other area resembling North America. For the rest of the world, the great majority of the societies have Possession Trance, ranging from 56% in the Circum-Mediterranean to 72% in East Eurasia, while Trance ranges from 36% in Africa and the Circum-Mediterranean to 60% in the Insular Pacific. Thus, the expectation derived from Old World data, that the number of societies with possession trance exceeds the number with trance, is not at all supported by the American data (Bourguignon 1968, 1973).

Much of what has been noted above indicates that North America is characterized by a predominance of hunting, gathering, and fishing societies, and also, generally, by less complex political and social systems. As we look beyond enumeration to correlational studies that differentiate among the regions of the world, we also find that some correlations which hold true worldwide or in other regions do not appear to hold true for North America. Several examples are cited below in our discussion of the implications of the present study. For now, we may note that the Americas have often been seen by anthropologists as a testing ground for theories developed on the basis of various types of Old World data. The similarities and differences between the Old and the New World with respect to the independent developments of plant and animal domestication, pottery, urban centers, and state organizations are well known. Kroeber (1962) catalogued presences and absences of cultural characteristics in the Old World and the New. More recently, Adams (1966) has presented a detailed and systematic comparison of the independent evolution of urban society in Early Mesopotamia and Prehispanic Mexico, finding few differences but an overwhelming number of similarities "in form and process" (Adams 1966: 174). In so doing, he brings up to date the development of the discussion of evolutionary regularities in the growth of urban civilizations, stemming from the work of Steward and Wittfogel.

Yet, in some respects, the differences cited here between, on the one hand, the Americas as a whole and North America in particular, and, on the other, the major ethnographic regions of the Old World remain a challenge to broad assumptions regarding worldwide similarities in evolutionary development of societies and functional relationships. This appears to be particularly true regarding the broad range of societies of lesser complexity than those we commonly refer to as "civilizations."

III

Implications and Conclusions

The implications of the findings of the present study fall roughly into three categories: the need for expanding basic source material, evaluation of generalizations in societal analysis, and implications for research methods.

Need for Expanding Basic Source Material

As is evident from the tables and as has been indicated in our earlier discussion, descriptive coverage of various societal characteristics is unequal in the ethnographic literature. This is the case even for the two world areas—Africa and North America—that are represented in the *Ethnographic Atlas* by the largest number of societies. It is hoped that the presentation of these data will encourage future investigators to fill the gaps in our knowledge not only with respect to inadequately studied geographic regions but also with respect to inadequately studied subjects in societies for which partial data—largely in the areas of subsistence economy and kinship organization—are now available. It should be noted that many vital aspects of society are not covered by the *Atlas* and, therefore, that extension both of ethnographic research and of *Atlas* coding to provide more complete data for all societies seems eminently desirable.

While fairly complete information is available on the details of subsistence economy—a subject which is covered more fully than any of the others treated here—other aspects of the economy, except for craft and industrial specialization, are completely lacking. Thus, for example, the *Atlas* does not include any data on trade, forms of economic organization, or levels of living, to mention a few. The information given on social structure, political organization, and religion generally concerns only one or two critical aspects of these important societal attributes. Details of the class structure, the use of power, effects of colonialization, and the nature of religious belief and its role in the life of the society are some examples of valuable data not coded at present. Information on several important aspects of kinship and marriage, generally of recurrent interest to anthropologists, are available. On the other hand, other important information in this area, such as size of family, marriage age, divorce, and birth control methods, which would also be of great interest, are not available. Some, but by no means all, social restrictions are covered, and only a limited amount of information is provided on the subject of games.

Since the appearance of the *Atlas* summary (Murdock 1967a), important coded data have been published for a selected group of 186 societies, which, according to Murdock and White (1969), are a representative sample of known world cultures. For this select group, additional information is now available on such economic factors as trade, transportation, and money and credit (Murdock and Morrow 1970); on infancy and early child-rearing practices (Barry and Paxson 1971); and on additional aspects of settlement and community organization (Murdock and Wilson 1972), as well as political organization (Tuden and Marshall 1972). While these valuable additions help to fill in the gaps in our knowledge, the need for such data on all societies included in the *Atlas* is still most important, since the value of using a small, selected sample of societies to represent the world's cultures remains open to question. Furthermore, if regional variations are to be investigated, a sample of 186 societies is, in fact, likely to be too small. Some thoughts on this will be discussed further on.

An important aspect of any societal study concerns change within the society. It would therefore be of great interest to know which societies are expanding and which are remaining relatively static or retrenching in terms of population, economic activity, political organization, and so forth. The *Atlas* data, coded for a particular time, necessarily present an impression of static groups. No data on change are included, though many, if not all, of the societies covered have experienced, continue to experience, or are starting to experience large-scale changes.

It is recognized that implementation of the suggestions made here presents difficulties both in locating the data and in devising suitable codes and categories for summarizing the information. The importance of the knowledge, however, seems great enough to warrant efforts both among those doing fieldwork and those working on codification procedures to expand their sights and provide greater and more uniform coverage than we have at present. The development of uniform standards for ethnographic research, as mentioned earlier, seems a logical and needed step.

Generalizations in Societal Analysis

A. The problem of regional variation. Since each of the major ethnographic regions of the world presents its own distinctive profile, there is an inherent difficulty in any generalization based on worldwide totals, for it necessarily obscures this distinctiveness in reducing broad ranges of variation to averages. In turn, the profiles of the major regions represent compromises among the culture areas of which they are composed. Some world areas, however, are more homogeneous or more heterogeneous than others, so that there is some variation among areas as to the amount of distortion involved in dealing with each of the six areas as defined in the *Atlas*.

An illustration of the first point, the danger of worldwide generalizations, has already been discussed in the previous chapter under Sex Division of Labor in Agriculture. Table 24, Belief in High Gods, offers another example. This table indicates that 21% of the coded societies world wide have a belief in a high god concerned with human morality. This total includes a broad range, from a maximum of 86% for the Circum-Mediterranean area to a minimum of 7% in South America. Such heterogeneity may exist within a given area as well. For example most of the societies of South America are coded as having shifting agriculture (70%), while 9% are coded as "casual," 3% as "horticulture," 7% as "intensive," and 11% as having no form of agriculture. Agriculture in South America is thus seen as running the gamut from "absent" to "intensive," with most of the societies in the middle range. The elements of this diversity with respect to types of agriculture in South America (as in other areas of the world) can easily be localized with respect to subregions or culture areas.

In respect to certain features, some regions appear to hold a virtual monopoly. A few examples may be cited: Horticulture appears to be practically limited to the Insular Pacific area; again, of all the seminomadic societies, 70% are in North America. Societies with three or four jurisdictional levels above the local level are totally absent in North America. Fully one-half of the societies with double descent are in Africa, while this type of descent is absent in North and South America. Seventy-three percent of all the societies coded that have complete segregation of adolescent boys are found in two of the six world areas: Africa and the Insular Pacific; while 81% of the societies for which male genital mutilation at any age is reported are found in Africa and in the Circum-Mediterranean area; of all societies reporting male genital mutilation between eleven and fifteen years of age, 70% are in Africa. On the other hand, this trait is totally unreported for both North and South America. And of all societies with ethical monotheism (belief in a high god concerned with morality), 57% are in the Circum-Mediterranean.

B. Generalizations and quantitative data. The existence of large amounts of quantitative data, such as those included in the *Ethnographic Atlas*, must necessarily affect the style as well as the content of sociological and anthropological generalizations, whether in theoretical discussions or in textbook presentations. In the past, unfortunately, it has often been necessary and, indeed, unavoidable to generalize on the basis of impressionistic information. Thus, in a context of examples, it is interesting to consider some instances of the generalizations that are found in the literature. In speaking of the "union of the husband, wife and their children," Lévi-Strauss (1956: 270) notes that "while such a group among us constitutes the family and is given legal recognition, this is by no means the case in a large number of human societies" and, further, "the great majority of societies, however, do not show a very active interest in [this] kind of grouping . . . " (Lévi-Strauss 1956: 271). According to our Table 28, Family Form, 50% of 856 societies in all parts of the world have the independent family; all areas, except East Eurasia and North America, are characterized by the nuclear family in more than 50% of their societies. And even in East Eurasia and North America, the percentage does not drop below 40%.

Other examples are not difficult to find: we read in the *Handbook of South American Indians*, under the heading of "The High Gods": "The tradition of a creator or Great Ancestor . . . is probably general throughout South America" (Métraux 1949: 559). The author warns us, however, that the "poor quality of the source materials at our disposal" makes a general statement about South American Indian religion most difficult. Our Table 24, Belief in High Gods, shows only sixty-seven societies coded with respect to this dimension for the entire continent. However, for 42% of these, a belief in a high god is coded as either absent or unreported.

With respect to residence rules, Ralph Linton (1936: 169) wrote: "Matrilineal descent is normally linked with matrilocal residence, patrilineal with patrilocal." Murdock (1949: 59) concurs in this generalization on the basis of data on 250 societies. However, a comparison of our Tables 30, Kin Groups, and 29, Marital Residence, presents a more refined breakdown. Following the *Ethnographic Atlas*, we distinguish between patrilocal and virilocal residence, grouped in the above-cited examples under the heading "patrilocal," and between matrilocal and uxorilocal residence, formerly combined under the heading of "matrilocal." Yet we find in three of the six world areas, i.e. Africa, the Circum-Mediterranean, and Insular Pacific, that the number and percentage of societies with patrilocal residence exceeds that of societies with patrilineal descent. In North America, however, forty-two societies (19%) have patrilineal descent, but only thirty (14%) have patrilocal residence. On the other hand, virilocal residence, which is relatively rare elsewhere, accounts for ninety-five North American societies, or 44% of the total. With respect to matrilineal descent, we find that in all world areas, the percentage of societies with matrilineal kin groups exceeds that of societies with either matrilocal, and/or avunculocal residence. If, however, we add the percentage of societies with uxorilocal residence to this total, the reverse is true. In South America, where only 8% of the societies are reported as having matrilineal kin groups, 40% have one of these three residence types. With 32% of its societies having uxorilocal residence, South America by far exceeds the worldwide average of 8% with respect to this characteristic. On the other hand, in the Circum-Mediterranean area, where only 7% of the societies have matrilineal kin groups, both matrilocal and uxorilocal residence are absent and only two societies (2%) have avunculocal residence.

It is clear that the large quantities of numerical data which are now available, however they are evaluated by the critical reader, must be taken into account in descriptive accounts and theoretical formulations. A beginning of such a new trend is already to be seen. Among sociologists, Lenski stands out as one who makes extensive use of comparative data from a broad range of societies in his introduction to sociology. He refers to the *Ethnographic Atlas* as the "richest source of systematic information on human societies" (Lenski 1970: 130). Specifically, Lenski summarizes the data on the 915 societies coded in the *Ethnographic Atlas* as of April 1966. He establishes a typology of human societies based on forms of subsistence and groups the data of the *Ethnographic Atlas* accordingly. Although he does not provide measures of association, he does present the data in relationship to his typology. The work of William Goode (1963) on world family patterns is also an excellent example of the careful use of generalizations based on vast quantities of source material, although from sources other than the *Ethnographic Atlas*. In social and cultural anthropology, some introductory textbooks have been utilizing statistical and quantitative data for more than a dozen years (e.g. Honigmann 1959, Hoebel 1966). The most extensive incorporation of such data is found in the most recent edition of Hoebel's well-known text (1972). Relying on Coult and Habenstein's work (1965) with the World Ethnographic Sample and on an earlier version of our own work (Bourguignon and Greenbaum 1968), as well as on some additional cross-cultural studies, Hoebel uses quantitative data to provide a framework of generalizations within which specific illustrations can be presented. As Hoebel puts it, quantitative data, permitting statements of exact frequency, are more desirable than "'rarely,' 'common,' or 'usually,' which have so long been characteristic of anthropological generalizations" (Hoebel 1972: 73). It thus appears that as a result of the readier availability of quantitative data there is indeed a tendency away from the reliance on a few examples as a support for broad generalizations or, indeed, as an end in themselves. While such presentations may have been unavoidable in the past because of a dearth of information, and have regrettably characterized much of the writing by sociologists and anthropologists directed toward beginning students, as well as to a larger lay and professional audience, this need not continue.

Implications for Research Design

Many of the correlation studies published in the last several years appear to have two distinct methodological handicaps. First, the value of the popular two-by-two table as a basis for statistical measurements of association or correlation can be seriously questioned on the basis of the data we have presented. To develop such two-by-two tables, polarities must be created. The pitfalls of this procedure may be seen in several of our tables, but most clearly perhaps in Table 27, Marriage Form. If we wish to contrast societies having monogamy with those having polygyny, we are confronted with the problem of where to assign the category "monogamy with occasional polygyny." We may group this category with that of monogamy, reasoning that here, too, the statistical norm is one of monogamy. If we do so, we obtain, on a worldwide basis, 55% monogamy versus 44% polygyny (polyandry being negligible in percentage terms). On the other hand, we might group "monogamy with occasional polygyny" with polygyny, on the basis that both of these categories reflect the norm of custom or law. Polygyny is permissible or even desirable in both of these categories of societies. If we thus combine the two forms of polygyny, we obtain the following results: 16% monogamy versus 83% polygyny. While some justification for both positions can be advanced, nevertheless either one would necessarily bias the results in the direction of some, perhaps unstated, assumptions. Before choosing to work with polar types, it appears desirable to begin with a larger number of categories and to collapse these into a smaller number only where, on the basis of a preliminary check of frequencies, polarities do not distort social facts and do not introduce hidden assumptions into the classification of the data and hence into the results of the analysis. Otherwise, polarities should be rejected in favor of several meaningful categories.

Along these lines, the recent work of Chaney, Morton, and Moore (1972) is instructive. They re-examined the Naroll and D'Andrade (1963) interval sift method to provide a solution to what has come to be known as "Galton's problem." Naroll and D'Andrade used dichotomized Residence Rules and Descent Rules, and were able by the sifting method to eliminate statistically significant effects of diffusion. When Chaney, Morton, and Moore subdivided Residence Rules and Descent Rules into three categories each, instead of two, they found that the sift method failed to produce consistently similar results. As they state it:

> The implication of the above is that the relationship for qualitative variables (if anything) is between the attributes rather than between the entire variable [Chaney, Morton, and Moore 1972: 223].

In other words, polarities may be deceptive in determining statistical relationships.

Second, the important fact of regional clustering of characteristics throws grave doubt on any causal inferences made on the basis of correlational studies which ignore this regional clustering. Broad correlational studies published to date (e.g. Coult and Habenstein 1965; Spiro 1965; Textor 1967), based as they are on two-by-two tables and seeking correlations generally on a world-wide rather than regional basis, have not as yet established their usefulness, either for ascertaining descriptive truths about societal characteristics or for expanding fruitful research in this field.

It will be noted that we have presented only distributions in the form of totals and percentages, and that we have not made any attempt at correlations. This was done in order to gain some understanding first of regional variation, as well as to provide a quantitative assessment of the available data. We have, however, explored elsewhere some possible correlation studies within regional areas, and we may briefly refer to some of this work, although its details do not fall within the scope of the present study. Our efforts along these lines have convinced us again not only of the importance of regional differences but also of the need for a depth of understanding of societal phenomena that goes beyond statistical findings. We wish to indicate here some of the problems we have discovered in seeking correlations of societal variables. Our findings in this respect are consistent with the work of some others along similar lines.

Thus, Driver and Schuessler (1967) found important differences in correlations between world areas in a correlation study of Murdock's World Ethnographic Sample, the greatest statistically significant differences being between North America and the Circum-Mediterranean area. They seek explanations for these differences in historical and ecological factors. They also see these differences as due in part to choice of variables and processes of sampling.

Greenbaum (n.d.) and LeVine (1960), working independently and with different samples, found that the significant correlations between stratification and levels of jurisdictional hierarchy in other ethnographic regions, do not exist in North America. It would seem, therefore, that to look at phenomena on a worldwide basis may not only not yield significant worldwide insights but can also obscure the more interesting and significant regional variations.

We employed a variation of the above research approach to our work on altered states of consciousness, mentioned previously. Here a typology of these states, termed "trance types," was developed on the basis of our own coding of data from the ethnographic literature. The variables involved in this typology were compared with variables derived from the *Ethnographic Atlas* and already available in the OSU Card File. This analysis provided some insight into the nature of societies with institutionalizations of different kinds of altered states. In this research we carried out correlations both on a worldwide basis and on a regional basis and found statistically significant correlations between our trance types and a series of twelve variables for a worldwide sample. These variables were concerned in part with societal complexity and showed that one type, possession trance, was significantly more likely to occur in more complex societies. However, we also found important regional differences, so that, for example, in North America only five of the twelve variables were significantly correlated with our trance types. We interpreted these regional differences as being related, in part, to diffusion and to the regional profiles which we discussed earlier (Bourguignon 1968, 1973).

In our study of the specific phenomenon of possession trance among societies of Sub-Saharan Africa, significant but puzzling correlations were discovered between the presence of possession trance and the presence of stratification and slavery (Greenbaum 1973a). Following the caveat that correlation does not mean causation, further library and statistical research focused on an interesting intervening variable, namely the degree of rigidity in the integration of a society as a correlate of both possession trance and of stratification and slavery (Greenbaum 1973b). Whether this relationship holds true for other geographic regions is still untested. It is felt, however, that a worldwide rather than a regional study of these phenomena would have been less likely to reveal the associations that appeared in the study of the African area.

These examples illustrate the reasons for our stressing the need for regional comparative studies in preference to worldwide correlations using two-by-two tables. They also give some idea of the wealth of possible future studies that might be fruitfully undertaken with the use of large quantities of coded ethnographic data.

Finally, a word on sampling for cross-cultural research is necessary. Much effort has been spent determining samples to eliminate diffusional effects, to solve for Galton's problem, and/ or to comply with stipulations by Murdock and others for representation of diverse cultural groups. Both Greenbaum (1970, n.d.) and Schaefer et al. (1971), working independently, have so far found no statistically significant differences between samples chosen randomly and those chosen by a stratified method to eliminate diffusion bias. This finding holds true for both frequency distributions and correlations of variables. Additional research is, of course, necessary for more definitive answers to the difficult question of sampling. Currently, however, the use either of the totality of societies as presented here or random sampling for specific studies has been established as a statistically sound approach in cross-cultural work.

Conclusion

The following quotations from Gunnar Myrdal's *Asian Drama* (1968) sum up in essence why we have attempted this book:

> The risk [of fundamental error] is heightened by the dearth of empirical data on social realities . . . [p. 17].

> . . . Although it is the confrontation with the facts that ultimately will rectify our conceptual apparatus, initially the paucity and flimsiness of data . . . leaves ample opportunity for biases, and the continuing collection of data under biased notions only postpones the day when reality can effectively challenge inherited preconceptions [p. 18].

> . . . Questions are necessarily prior to answers, and no answers are conceivable that are not answers to questions. A "purely factual" study—observation of a segment of social reality with no preconceptions—is not possible; it could only lead to a chaotic accumulation of meaningless impressions . . . Scientific data—facts established by observation and classification—have no existence outside the framework of preconceptions. Generalizations about reality, and their organization within an abstract framework of presumed interrelations, precede specification and verification. They constitute "theory" in research [p. 24].

> . . . But it is also a first principle of science that facts are sovereign. Theory, therefore, must not only be subjected to immanent criticism for logical consistency, but must constantly be measured against reality and adjusted accordingly [p. 24].

> The two processes go together. As we increase the volume of observational data to which we are led by our analytical preconceptions, our original theories are refitted in order to make sense of the data and explain them. This is the crux of all science . . . [p. 24-25].

We hope our efforts to present and analyze a body of data have in some way helped to reduce the "dearth of empirical data on social realities." We have raised some questions to "challenge inherited preconceptions." We have urged against a "chaotic accumulation of meaningless impressions" and for a regional framework of conception and research design in cross-cultural studies. We recognize further the need for constant interplay between theories and observational data and hope that whatever we may have added of value here will be examined and re-examined, added to, revised, and superseded in the future to advance the scientific study of human societies.

References

Adams, Robert McC.

1966   *The evolution of urban society: Early Mesopotamia and Prehispanic Mexico,* Chicago, Aldine.

Barry, Herbert, III, and Leonora M. Paxson

1971   "Infancy and early childhood: cross-cultural codes 2," *Ethnology 10:* 466-508.

Bourguignon, Erika

1968   *A cross-cultural study of dissociational states: final report,* Columbus, Ohio State University Research Foundation.

1973   Introduction: "A framework for the comparative study of altered states of consciousness," in Erika Bourguignon, ed., *Religion, Altered States of Consciousness and Social Change,* Columbus, Ohio State University Press: 3-35.

Bourguignon, Erika, and Lenora Greenbaum
1968   *Diversity and homogeneity: a comparative analysis of societal characteristics based on data from the Ethnographic Atlas,* Occasional Paper, Number One, Department of Anthropology, Columbus, Ohio State University.

Chaney, Richard P., Keith Morton, and Turrall Moore

1972   "On the entangled problems of selection and conceptual organization," *American Anthropologist 74:* 221-30.

Coult, Allen D., and Robert W. Habenstein

1965   *Cross-tabulations of Murdock's World Ethnographic Sample,* Columbia, University of Missouri.

Driver, Harold E., and Karl F. Schuessler

   1967   "Correlational analysis of Murdock's 1957 ethnographic sample," *American Anthropologist 69*: 332-52.

Evans-Pritchard, E. E.

   1971   "Sources, with particular reference to the Southern Sudan," *Cahiers d'Études Africaines 11*: 129-79.

French, David

   1963   "The relationship of anthropology to studies in perception and cognition," in S. Koch, ed., *Psychology: A Study of a Science, Study 2, Vol. 6,* New York, McGraw-Hill: 388-428.

Goode, William J.

   1963   *World revolution and family patterns,* New York, Free Press.

Greenbaum, Lenora

   n.d.   *Statistical probabilities, functional relationships, and Galton's problem: a summary of ongoing research,* paper presented at the 1973 Annual Meeting of the American Anthropological Association.

   1970   "Evaluation of a stratified versus an unstratified universe of cultures in comparative research," *Behavior Science Notes 5*: 251-89.

   1973a "Societal correlates of possession trance in sub-Saharan Africa," in Erika Bourguignon, ed., *Religion, Altered States of Consciousness and Social Change,* Columbus, Ohio State University Press.

   1973b "Possession trance in sub-Saharan Africa: a descriptive analysis of fourteen societies," in Erika Bourguignon, ed., *Religion, Altered States of Consciousness and Social Change,* Columbus, Ohio State University Press: 58-87.

Hanks, Lucien M., Jr., and Jane R. Hanks

   1964   "Siamese Tai," in Frank L. LeBar, Gerald C. Hickey, and John M. Musgrave, eds., *Ethnic Groups of Mainland Southeast Asia,* New Haven, HRAF Press: 197-205.

Hoebel, E. Adamson

1966   *Anthropology*, New York, McGraw-Hill.

1972   *Anthropology* (4th ed.), New York, McGraw-Hill.

Honigmann, John J.

1959   *The world of man*, New York, Harper and Brothers.

Köbben, André J. F.

1967   "Why exceptions? The logic of cross-cultural analysis," *Current Anthropology 8*: 3-34.

Kroeber, Alfred L.

1962   "A roster of civilization and culture," *Viking Fund Publications in Anthropology 33*.

Lenski, Gerhard

1970   *Human societies: a macrolevel introduction to sociology*, New York, McGraw-Hill.

Lévi-Strauss, Claude

1956   "The family," in H. Shapiro, ed., *Man, Culture and Society*, New York, Oxford University Press: 261-85.

LeVine, Robert A.

1960   "The role of the family in authority systems: a cross-cultural application of stimulus-generalization theory," *Behavioral Science 5*: 291-96.

Linton, Ralph

1936   *The study of man*, New York, Appleton-Century.

Métraux, Alfred

1949   "Religion and shamanism," in Julian H. Steward, ed., *Handbook of South American Indians 5, Bulletin of the Bureau of American Ethnology 143*: 559-99.

Murdock, George Peter

  1949   *Social structure,* New York, Macmillan.

  1957   "World ethnographic sample," *American Anthropologist*
          59: 664-87.

  1966   "Cross-cultural sampling," *Ethnology* 5: 97-114.

  1967a   "Ethnographic atlas: a summary," *Ethnology* 6: 109-236.

  1967b   *Ethnographic atlas,* Pittsburgh, University of Pittsburgh
          Press.

Murdock, George Peter, and Diana O. Morrow

  1970   "Subsistence economy and supportive practices: cross-cul-
          tural codes 1," *Ethnology 9*: 302-30.

Murdock, George Peter, and Douglas R. White

  1969   "Standard cross-cultural sample," *Ethnology 8*: 329-69.

Murdock, George Peter, and Suzanne F. Wilson

  1972   "Settlement patterns and community organization: cross-
          cultural codes 2," *Ethnology II*: 254-95.

Murdock, George Peter, et al.

  1962   "Ethnographic atlas," *Ethnology 1 to date.*

  1969   *Outline of cultural materials,* 4th rev. ed., 4th printing,
          with modifications, New Haven, Human Relations Area
          Files.

Myrdal, Gunnar

  1968   *Asian drama: an inquiry into the poverty of nations,* New
          York, Pantheon Books.

Naroll, Raoul

  1962   *Data quality control—a new research technique: prolego-
          mena to a cross-cultural study of culture stress,* New York,
          Free Press of Glencoe.

  1964   "On ethnic unit classification," *Current Anthropology 5*:
          283-312.

  1970a   "Data quality control in cross-cultural surveys," in Raoul
          Naroll and Ronald Cohen, eds., *A Handbook of Method
          in Cultural Anthropology,* Garden City, Natural History
          Press: 927-45.

1970b "The culture-bearing unit in cross-cultural surveys," in Raoul Naroll and Ronald Cohen, eds., *A Handbook of Method in Cultural Anthropology*, Garden City, Natural History Press: 721-65.

Naroll, Raoul, and Roy G. D'Andrade

1963 "Two further solutions to Galton's problem," *American Anthropologist 65*: 1053-67.

Naroll, Raoul, et al.

1970 "Standard ethnographic sample," *Current Anthropology 11*: 235-48.

Schaefer, James M., et al.

1971 "Sampling methods, functional associations and Galton's problem: a replicative assessment," *Behavior Science Notes 6*: 229-74.

Spiro, Melford E.

1965 "A typology of social structure and the patterning of social distributions: a cross-cultural study," *American Anthropologist 67*: 1097-1119.

Swanson, Guy E.

1960 *The birth of the gods: the origin of primitive beliefs*, Ann Arbor, University of Michigan Press.

Textor, Robert B.

1967 *A cross-cultural summary*, New Haven, HRAF Press.

Tuden, Arthur, and Catherine Marshall

1972 "Political organization: cross-cultural codes 4," *Ethnology 11:* 436-64.

Vallier, Ivan, ed.

1971 *Comparative methods in sociology: essays on trends and applications*, Berkeley, University of California Press.

APPENDIX I

The Ohio State University
Punched Card File of
Ethnographic Data:

Code Book

Appendix I

The Ohio State University Punched Card File of Ethnographic Data is the source of all statistical tabulations of world societies contained in this volume. The basic data for this card file were taken from the *Ethnographic Atlas;* all societies coded in its summary have been included here.

All information on societal characteristics contained in the *Atlas* appears on the OSU File cards, with the exception of the following indicators:

Most lower-case codes, indicating alternative or secondary practices

Asterisks and other markings

Also, the following categories have been omitted from consideration:

Kinship Terminology for Cousins

Linguistic Affiliation

Caste Stratification

Inheritance of Real and Movable Property

House Type

Definitions are taken from their first appearance in the *Ethnographic Atlas*, starting with its first installment (Murdock et. al. 1962-). Occasionally, where wording was changed in the *Ethnographic Atlas* Summary (Murdock 1967a, 1967b), preference was given to the latter text.

For most societal characteristics, the categories of the *Atlas* have been combined, with the result that the OSU File contains fewer but larger categories than the *Atlas*. Coding of the information for the OSU File has been changed from alphabetic to numeric symbols. The card form has been redesigned, and related societal characteristics have been grouped together.

The following code listings are presented to make possible detailed comparison of the data in the OSU File with those the *Ethnographic Atlas*. For all category and coding revision an explanation is given to clarify both our method and our re sons for the changes introduced in the OSU File.

In these explanations, occasional reference is made to the u of Blaine's cards. This means that frequencies were determin by using a set of 604 cards prepared by Harry Blaine of The Oh State University, based on the material contained in the *Ethno graphic Atlas* as of 1964. These frequencies were an importa guide in our decisions concerning category revision and conso dation.

The presentation of codes follows the sequence of material the cards of the OSU File. This substantially matches the quence of statistical tabulations presented in this volume.

EA   CODE DEFINITION
Col. Code

1   *Six Major Ethnographic Areas*

A   Africa, exclusive of Madagascar and the north-
     ern and northeastern portions of the continent.

C   Circum-Mediterranean, including Europe, Turkey
     and the Caucasus, the Semitic Near East, and
     northern and northeastern Africa.

E   East Eurasia, excluding Formosa, the Philippines,
     Indonesia, and the area assigned to the Circum-
     Mediterranean but including Madagascar and
     other islands in the Indian Ocean.

I   Insular Pacific, embracing all of Oceania as well
     as areas like Australia, Indonesia, Formosa,
     and the Philippines that are not always included
     therewith.

N   North America, including the indigenous societies
     of this continent as far south as the Isthmus
     of Tehuantepec.

S   South America, including the Antilles, Yucatan
     and Central America as well as the continent
     itself.

SU File l. Code	EA Col. Code	CODE DEFINITION	EXPLANATION OF CATEGORY REVISION
	1	*Six Major Ethnographic Areas*	
1	A	Africa	Each defined as in the *Atlas*. No change.
2	C	Circum-Mediterranean	
3	E	East Eurasia	
4	I	Insular Pacific	
5	N	North America	
6	S	South America	

DEFINITION OF CODES USED IN EA

CODE DEFINITION

EA Col. Code

2

Ten Lesser Regions

	Africa	Circum-Med.	E. Eurasia	Ins. Pac.	N. America	S. America
a	African Hunters	Ethiopia & the Horn	Middle East	Philippines & Formosa	Arctic America	Central America
b	South African Bantu	Muslim Sudan	Central Asia	Western Indonesia	Northwest Coast	Caribbean
c	Central Bantu	Sahara	Arctic Asia	Eastern Indonesia	California	Guiana
d	Northeast Bantu	North Africa	East Asia	Australia	Great Basin & Plateau	Lower Amazon
e	Equatorial Bantu	Southern Europe	Himalayas	New Guinea	Plains	Interior Amazonia
f	Guinea Coast	Overseas Europeans	North & Central India	Micronesia	Prairie	Andes
g	Western Sudan	Northwestern Europe	South India	Western Melanesia	Eastern Woodlands	Chile & Patagonia
h	Nigerian Plateau	Eastern Europe	Indian Ocean	Eastern Melanesia	Southwest	Gran Chaco
i	Eastern Sudan	Turkey & Caucasus	Assam & Burma	Western Polynesia	Northwest Mexico	Mato Grosso
j	Upper Nile	Semitic Near East	Southeast Asia	Eastern Polynesia	Central Mexico	Eastern Brazil

J File Code	*EA Col.*	*Code*	CODE DEFINITION	EXPLANATION OF CATEGORY REVISION
	2		*Ten Lesser Regions*	
0		a		Each as defined in the *Atlas*. No change.
1		b		
2		c		
3		d		
4		e		
5		f		
6		g		
7		h		
8		i		
9		j		
			Code Number of the Society	No change.
			Name of the Society	First five letters of the Society's name. Some common sense abbreviations however, have been made. For example, French Canadian is coded FRCAN; Plateau Tonga is coded PTONG; Bella Bella is coded BELLA, while Bella Coola is coded COOLA.

EA   CODE DEFINITION
Col. Code

Subsistence Economy

7   *Gathering of Wild Plants and Small Land Faun*

        0   Zero to 5% dependence

        1   6 to 15% dependence

        2   16 to 25% dependence

        3   26 to 35% dependence

        4   36 to 45% dependence

        5   46 to 55% dependence

        6   56 to 65% dependence

        7   66 to 75% dependence

        8   76 to 85% dependence

        9   86 to 100% dependence

8   *Hunting, Including Trapping and Fowling*
                      Same as under *Gathering*

9   *Fishing, Including Shellfishing and the Pursu*
                      of Large Aquatic Animals
                      Same as under *Gathering*

10   *Animal Husbandry*
                      Same as under *Gathering*

11   *Agriculture*
                      Same as under *Gathering*

File Code	EA Col.	Code	CODE DEFINITION	EXPLANATION OF CATEGORY REVISION
			SUBSISTENCE ECONOMY	
	7		*Gathering of Wild Plants and Small Land Fauna*	For each of the five areas, Gathering, Hunting, Fishing, Animal Husbandry, and Agriculture, the nine categories of
1		0, 1, 2	0 to 25% dependence	the *Atlas* have been condensed into four.
2		3,4	26 to 45% dependence	Each category indicates a range of 20% to 30% in the socie-
3		5,6,7	46 to 75% dependence	ties' dependence on the particular activ-
4		8,9	76 to 100% dependence	ity, instead of about 10% as in the *Atlas*.
	8		*Hunting, Including Trapping and Fowling* Same as under *Gathering*	
	9		*Fishing, Including Shellfishing and the Pursuit of Large Aquatic Animals* Same as under *Gathering*	
	10		*Animal Husbandry* Same as under *Gathering*	
	11		*Agriculture* Same as under *Gathering*	

J File Code	*EA Col. Code*	CODE DEFINITION	EXPLANATION OF CATEGORY REVISION
	7,8,9	*Gathering, Hunting, and Fishing*	

For each society, the *EA* codes in *EA* Columns 7, 8, and 9 have been added together. The total dependence on *Gathering, Hunting,* and *Fishing* combined is coded:

Little or no dependence on these activities. Sum of codes = 0 or 1 or 2

2 — Moderately low dependence on these activities. Sum of codes = 3 or 4

3 — Moderately heavy dependence on these activities. Sum of codes = 5 or 6

4 — Heavy dependence on these activities. Sum of codes = 7 or 8 or 9 or 10

Some effort is made here to determine the overall picture of the Subsistence Economy. Hence, the *EA* codes in Columns 7, 8, and 9 have been added together. The sum of these codes has been indicated on the cards of OSU File. This indicates the degree of the society's dependence on Gathering, Hunting, and Fishing combined. The survival of some societies depends on this combination, though the dependence on any one may not be strikingly great.

U File Code	*EA Col. Code*	CODE DEFINITION	EXPLANATION OF CATEGORY REVISION
	10,11	*Animal Husbandry and Agriculture*	
1	3 or higher in both columns	Between 52 and 100% dependence on Animal Husbandry and Agriculture combined, *where there exists at least 26% dependence on* each one.	Some societies depend on a combination of Animal Husbandry and Agriculture. To capture information on those that depend largely on both but not exclusively on one or the other, information is noted on OSU File cards to show those societies that depend on Animal Husbandry and Agriculture, each for at least 26% of their subsistence or more. These societies therefore depend on the combined activities of Animal Husbandry and Agriculture at least 52% or more, and on each one of these activities at least 26%.
2	0,1, or 2 in one or both columns	Society depends less than 25% on Animal Husbandry and/or less than 25% on Agriculture.	

EA	**CODE DEFINITION**
Col. Code	

28   *Type and Intensity of Agriculture*

C   Casual agriculture, i.e. the cultivation of a few
food or other plants incidental to a primary dependence upon other forms of subsistence
economy. An example would be a nomadic people who plant a few seeds at one season of the
year and return at another season to harvest
the scanty crop.

E   Extensive or shifting agriculture, i.e. where new
fields are cleared annually, cultivated for a year
or two, and then allowed to revert to forest or
brush for a long fallow period.

H   Horticulture, i.e. semi-intensive agriculture limited
mainly to small vegetable gardens or groves
of fruit trees rather than to the cultivation of
field crops.

I   Intensive agriculture on permanent fields, utilizing fertilization by compost or animal manure,
crop rotation, or other techniques so that fal-
lowing is unnecessary or is confined to relatively
short periods.

J   Intensive agriculture where it is largely dependent
upon irrigation.

O   Complete absence of agriculture.

U File Code	EA Col. Code	CODE DEFINITION	EXPLANATION OF CATEGORY REVISION
	28	*Type and Intensity of Agriculture*	
1	C	Casual agriculture	The six categories of the *Atlas* were combined into five.
2	E	Shifting agriculture	
3	H	Horticulture	
4	I, J	Intensive agriculture	The two categories indicating Intensive Agriculture, one with agriculture techniques, and the other with irrigation, were combined into one category.
5	O	Complete absence of agriculture	
0	Blank	No information	

EA   CODE DEFINITION
Col. Code

28 (cont.)   *Type and Intensity of Agriculture* (cont.)

> The second, or lower-case, symbol, indicates the principal type of food crop under the following categories:

c   Cereal grains, e.g. maize, millet, rice, or wheat the principal food crop or at least as important as any other type of crop.

n   Nonfood crops only, e.g. cotton or tobacco.

r   Roots or tubers, e.g. manioc, potato, taro, or yam the principal food crops or at least as importan as tree crops or vegetables and more importan than cereal grains.

t   Tree fruits, e.g. bananas, breadfruit, coconuts or dates, the principal food crops. Sago, unles specifically reported to be cultivated, is treatec as a gathered rather than as a cultivated fooc product.

v   Vegetables, e.g. cucurbits, greens, or legumes the principal food plants.

U File *Code*	*EA* *Col. Code*	CODE DEFINITION	EXPLANATION OF CATEGORY REVISION
ont.)	28 (cont.)	*Type and Intensity of Agriculture* (cont.)	
			The lower-case codes indicating the principal type of food crop were omitted.

EA

CODE DEFINITION

Col. Code

39-41   *Type of Animal Husbandry*
             (The capital letters denote the predominant
             type of domestic animals kept in the particular
             society. The smaller animals, e.g. pigs and sheep,
             will be indicated only when larger animals are
             absent or unimportant in the economy.)

B   Bovine animals, e.g. cattle, mithun, water buf-
      faloes, yaks.

C   Camels or other animals of related genera, e.g.
      alpacas, llamas.

D   Deer, e.g. reindeer.

E   Equine animals, e.g. horses, donkeys.

O   Absence or near absence of domestic animals
      other than bees, cats, dogs, fowl, guinea pigs
      or the like.

P   Pigs the only domestic animals of consequence.

S   Sheep and/or goats in the absence of important
      larger domestic animals.

             (A preposited lower-case *p* indicates the
      animals were employed in plow cultivation prior
      to the contact period; a lower-case *q* indicates
      that plow cultivation, though not aboriginal, was
      well established at the period of observation. A
      postposited lower-case *m* indicates that domestic
      animals are milked other than sporadically;
      lower-case *o* indicates the absence or near absence
      of milking.)

U File Code	EA Col. Code	CODE DEFINITION	EXPLANATION OF CATEGORY REVISION
	40	*Type of Animal Husbandry*	
1	B	Bovine animals	The seven codes were combined into six. Camels and equine were combined into one category because both are mounts. Otherwise the categories remained unchanged.
2	C,E	Camels, etc. and equine animals	
3	D	Deer, e.g. reindeer	
4	P	Pigs	
5	S	Sheep and/or goats only	
6	O	Absence or near absence of domestic animals	
0	Blank	No information	Lower-case codes indicating plow cultivation and milking have been omitted.

EA	CODE DEFINITION
Col. Code	

42-63   *Sex Division of Labor and Level of Technology*
Each technological and economic activity is assigned a separate column, but a single code is used for all activities and columns. This consists of a single capital letter, followed in some instances by a lower-case letter. The symbols employed are the following:

D   Differentiation of specific tasks by sex but approximately equal participation by both sexes in the total activity.

E   Equal participation in the activity by both sexes without marked or reported differentiation in specific tasks.

F   Females alone perform the activity, male participation being negligible or absent.

G   Both sexes participate, but females do appreciably more than males.

File Code	*EA Col. Code*	CODE DEFINITION	EXPLANATION OF CATEGORY REVISIONS
	42-63	*Sex Division of Labor*	
	54	*Gathering of Wild Plants and Small Land Fauna*	
		Where *EA* Column 7 is coded 0, 1, 2, 3, or 4, then:	Sex Division of Labor and Level of Technology are treated under two separate headings. The Sex Division of Labor
1	D,E	Equal participation	was included for the
2	F,G	Female labor predominates	five subsistence economy types, but not
3	M,N	Male labor predominates	for nonsubsistence
4	P,I	Sex not specified	activities. The latter have been omitted.

| *EA* | CODE DEFINITION |
| *Col. Code* | |

42-63   *Sex Division of Labor and Level of Technology*
(cont.)

I   Sex participation irrelevant, especially when
production is industrialized.

M   Males alone perform the activity, female partici
pation being negligible or absent.

N   Both sexes participate, but males do appreciabl
more than females.

O   The activity is absent or unimportant in the par
ticular society.

P   The activity is present, but sex participation i
unspecified in the sources consulted.

When not followed by a lower-case letter, th
foregoing symbols imply that the activity, if pres
ent in the culture, is normally performed by man
or most adult men, women, or both. Specializa
tion by age or occupational status, where reporte
to be present, is indicated by one of the followin
symbols in lower case:

SU File Code	EA Col. Code	CODE DEFINITION	EXPLANATION OF CATEGORY REVISION
	54	*Gathering of Wild Plants and Small Land Fauna* (cont.)	
		Where *EA* Column 7 is coded 5, 6, 7, 8, or 9 then: Equal participation	In utilizing the data on Sex Division of Labor, the eight *Atlas* codes were combined into four codes: equal participation (*Atlas* codes D and E) female predominates (*Atlas* codes F and G), male predominates (*Atlas* codes M and N), and sex not specialized or irrelevant (*Atlas* codes P and I). In using these codes, it was felt important to know not only the sex division of labor but simultaneously how important that activity was in the society.
5	D,E		
6	F,G	Female labor predominates	
7	M, N	Male labor predominates	
8	P,I	Sex not specified, or sex irrelevant, production industrialized	
9	O	No information or not important	
0	Blank	No information	

EA
CODE DEFINITION
Col. Code

42-63   *Sex Division of Labor and Level of Technology*
(cont.)

a   Senior age specialization, i.e. the activity is largely
performed by men and/or women beyond the
prime of life.

b   Junior age specialization, i.e. the activity is largely
performed by boys and/or girls before the age
of puberty.

c   Craft specialization, i.e. the activity is largely
performed by a small minority of adult males
or females who possess specialized skills. Occupational castes are treated as instances of
craft specialization.

i   Industrial specialization, i.e. the activity is largely
removed from the domain of a division of labor
by sex, age, or craft specialization and is performed mainly by industrialized techniques of
production.

(It remains to define the several columns to
which the above sets of symbols are applied.)

42   *Metal Working.* Only such arts as smelting,
casting, and forging, which involve the application of fire, will be indicated.

44   *Weaving.* Only the manufacture of true cloth on
a loom or frame will be indicated—not the manufacture of nets, baskets, mats, or nonwoven
fabrics like barkcloth or felt.

U File Code	EA Col.	Code	CODE DEFINITION	EXPLANATION OF CATEGORY REVISIONS
56			*Hunting, Including Trapping and Fowling* (same as under *Gathering*; refer to *EA* Column 8 for extent of *Hunting*).	In our coding we assigned one column to each subsistence economy activity. In that column we provided eight possible codes. The first four codes indicate the sex division of labor for societies where the particular activity is a minor activity in the society (coded 0 through 4 in one of the appropriate Columns 7 through 11).
58			*Fishing, Including Shellfishing and the Pursuit of Large Aquatic Animals* (same as under *Gathering*; refer to *EA* Column 9 for extent of *Fishing*).	
60			*Animal Husbandry* (same as under *Gathering*; refer to *EA* Column 10 for extent of *Animal Husbandry*).	The second four codes indicate the sex division of labor where the activity is a major societal activity (coded 5 through 9 in the appropriate *Atlas* Columns 7 through 11).
62			*Agriculture* (same as under *Gathering*; refer to *EA* Column 11 for extent of *Agriculture*).	We have omitted any indication of age specialization as shown by lower-case letters in the *Atlas'* coding.

EA	CODE DEFINITION
Col. Code	

42-63   *Sex Division of Labor and Level of Technology* (cont.)

46   *Leather Working.* Only the dressing of skins e.g. by tanning, will be indicated, not the manufacture of artifacts from raw hides or undressed skins.

48   *Pottery.* Only the manufacture of earthenware utensils will be indicated.

50   *Boat Building.* Only the construction of true water craft will be indicated, not the making of simple floats or the like.

52   *House Construction.* Only the actual building or erection of a dwelling will be indicated, not the acquisition or preliminary preparation of the materials used.

54   *Gathering.* For the definition of this and subsequent subsistence activities, see the code for Columns 7 through 11.

56   *Hunting.*

58   *Fishing.*

60   *Animal Husbandry.*

62   *Agriculture.*

SU File Code	EA Col. Code	CODE DEFINITION	EXPLANATION OF CATEGORY REVISION
	42-63	*Level of Technology*	
	43,45,47, 49,51,53, 55,57,59, 61,63	*Craft Specialization*	Craft specialization for all activities, both subsistence and non-subsistence, are indicated in the *Atlas* by a lower case "c" following the activity coded. To get some idea of the amount of craft specialization in a society, all the "c" codes were added together, and the total punched in one column. Any total over nine is included in the nine category. This permits usage of only one column for this information.
1,2,3 4,5,6 7,8,9	c	Number of craft specializations (total number of "c" codes in *EA* columns indicated)	
Blank		No "c" in any column	
	43,45,47, 49,51,53, 55,57,59, 61,63	*Industrial Specialization*	All "i" codes were added together, and the total punched in one column, following the same procedure described above for "c" codes.
,2,3, ,5,6, ,8,9	i	Number of industrial specializations (total number of "i" codes in *EA* columns indicated)	
lank		No "i" in any column	

EA		CODE DEFINITION
Col.	*Code*	

30   *Settlement Pattern*

B   Fully migratory or nomadic bands.

H   Separated hamlets where several such form a more or less permanent single community.

N   Neighborhoods of dispersed family homesteads.

S   Seminomadic communities whose members wander in bands for at least half of the year but occupy a fixed settlement at some season or seasons, e.g. recurrently occupied winter quarters.

T   Semisedentary communities whose members shift from one to another fixed settlement at different seasons or who occupy more or less permanently a single settlement from which, however, a substantial proportion of the population departs seasonally to occupy shifting camps, e.g. during transhumance.

V   Compact and relatively permanent settlements, i.e. nucleated villages or towns.

W   Compact but impermanent settlements, i.e. villages whose location is shifted every few years.

X   Complex settlements consisting of a nucleated village or town with outlying homesteads or satellite hamlets. Urban aggregations of population will not be separately indicated since Column 31 deals with community size.

SU File l. Code	EA Col. Code	CODE DEFINITION	EXPLANATION OF CATEGORY REVISION
	30	*Settlement Pattern*	
1	B	Migratory or nomadic bands	The eight *Atlas* categories were combined into five as follows: codes H and N, separated hamlets and dispersed homesteads, were combined into one code since both are scattered neighborhoods; seminomadic (code S) and semisedentary (code T) were combined into one; and compact permanent (code V) and complex (code X) were combined into one. The others remained the same.
2	H,N	Scattered neighborhoods	
3	S,T	Seminomadic or semisedentary communities	
4	V,X	Compact, complex, permanent settlements	
5	W	Compact, impermanent settlements	
0	Blank	No information	

EA
Col. Code   CODE DEFINITION

67-68   *Class Stratification*

C   Complex stratification into social classes cor-
     related in large measure with extensive differen-
     tiation of occupational statuses.

D   Dual stratification into a hereditary aristocracy
     and a lower class of ordinary commoners or free-
     men, where traditionally ascribed noble status
     is at least as decisive as the control over scarce
     resources and may even determine the latter.

E   Elite stratification, in which an elite class de-
     rives its superior status from, and perpetuates
     it through, control over scarce resources, par-
     ticularly land, and is thereby differentiated
     from a propertyless proletariat or serf class.

O   Absence of significant class distinctions among
     freemen, ignoring variations in individual repute
     achieved through skill, valor, piety, or wisdom.

W   Wealth distinctions, based on the possession or
     distribution of property, present and socially
     important but not crystallized into distinct
     and hereditary social classes.

     (In instances where the prevailing system of
     class stratification exhibits important features of
     two of the types defined above, this is indicated
     by combining a capital and a lower-case letter,
     e.g. Cd or Ec.)

SU File l. Code	EA Col. Code	CODE DEFINITION	EXPLANATION OF CATEGORY REVISION
	67	*Class Stratification*	
1	O	Absence of stratification of freemen and of slavery (where Column 71 contains code O)	These categories were combined with the categories in Columns 71-72, *Slavery*. The slavery codes were combined in such a way to indicate the presence or absence of slavery only. No further category breakdown on slavery was kept. Among the Class Stratification codes, Dual Stratification and Elite Stratification were combined into one category. These both concern societies where freemen are divided largely into two stratified groups. Each code for the stratification of freemen was then combined with a code for either the absence or presence of slavery.
2	O	Freemen and slaves (where Column 71 contains code H, I, or S)	
3	W	Wealth distinctions, no slavery (where Column 71 contains code O)	
4	W	Wealth distinctions, and slavery (where Column 71 contains code H, I, or S)	
5	D or E	Dual and elite stratification, no slavery (where Column 71 contains code O)	

EA   CODE DEFINITION

Col. Code

Class Stratification (cont.)

71-72   *Slavery.* Slave status is here treated entirely in-
               dependently of both class and caste status. Its
               forms and prevalence are indicated by the fol-
               lowing symbols:

     H   Hereditary slavery present and of at least modest
               social significance.

     I   Incipient or nonhereditary slavery, i.e. where slave
               status is temporary and not transmitted to the
               children of slaves.

     O   Absence or near absence of slavery.

     S   Slavery reported but not identified as hereditary or
               nonhereditary.

               (A postposited *f* indicates that slavery, though
               no longer practiced at the time level specified in
               "Classification into Clusters," had existed at an
               earlier period.)

SU File *)l. Code*	*EA* *Col. Code*	**CODE DEFINITION**	**EXPLANATION OF CATEGORY REVISION**
	67	*Class Stratification* (cont.)	
6	D or E	Dual and elite strati-fication, and slavery (where Column 71 contains code H, I, or S)	
7	C	Complex stratifica-tion, no slavery (where Column 71 contains code O)	
8	C	Complex stratifica-tion, and slavery (where Column 71 contains code H, I, or S)	
0	Blank	No information in either or both *EA* columns	
	71-72	*Slavery*	This has already been described above under *Class Stratifi-fication*. (All lower-case letters are omit-ted.)

EA
Col. Code

CODE DEFINITION

73   *Succession to the Office of Local Headman*

A   Nonhereditary succession through appointment by some higher political authority.

C   Nonhereditary succession through informal consensus.

E   Nonhereditary succession through election or some other method of formal consensus.

I   Nonhereditary succession through influence, e.g. of wealth or social status.

M   Hereditary succession by a sister's son.

N   Hereditary succession by a matrilineal heir who takes precedence over a sister's son, e.g. a younger brother.

O   Absence of any office resembling that of a local headman.

P   Hereditary succession by a son.

Q   Hereditary succession by a patrilineal heir who takes precedence over a son, e.g. a younger brother.

S   Nonhereditary succession on the basis primarily of seniority or age.

SU File i. Code	EA Col. Code	CODE DEFINITION	EXPLANATION OF CATEGORY REVISION
0	73	*Succession to the Office of Local Headman* *Nonhereditary Succession*	
1	A,I, S	By appointment, influence, seniority	The nine *Atlas* codes were combined into five categories, the division being by hereditary versus nonhereditary succession, each with two possible forms; and one code for no office of headman.
2	C,E	By election, consensus	
3	M,N	*Hereditary Succession* Matrilineal heir	
4	P,Q	Patrilineal heir	
5	O	Absence of office of headman	
0	Blank	No information	

EA		CODE DEFINITION
Col.	*Code*	

32-33   *Jurisdictional Hierarchy*

0   This column is derived from the codes on the
          number and typology of "sovereign organizations"
1   with which Swanson (1960) obtained highly il-
          luminating results in his study of religion. Our
          definition of jurisdictional levels coincides close-
2   ly with his definition of organizations character-
          ized by sovereignty, i.e. by original and definitive
3   jurisdiction over some sphere of social life in
          which the organization has the legitimate right
4   to make decisions having a significant effect on
          its members, e.g. distribution of food, allocation
          of productive resources, punishment of delicts,
          assignment or conscription of labor, levying of
          taxes, initiation of war or peace. Like Swanson,
          we exclude organizations that are merely agents
          of others and those not held to be legitimate (in-
          cluding colonial regimes and others imposed by
          force), and we always include the nuclear family
          and the local community in default of explicit evi-
          dence that they lack sovereignty in the defined
          sense. We differ from him mainly in insisting
          that such organizations fall into a single hier-
          archical order; we would, for example, count a
          lineage and its localized equivalent or clan as only
          a single jurisdictional level, not as two organiza-
          tions.

SU File ʲl. Code	EA Col. Code	CODE DEFINITION	EXPLANATION OF CATEGORY REVISION
	32-33	*Jurisdictional Hierarchy*	
		Two local levels (where *EA* Column 32 contains code 2) and:	The *Atlas* uses two columns to indicate (1) the number of jurisdictional levels up to the local level (Column 32) and (2) the number of levels beyond the local level (Column 33). We have combined these two and provided a set of eight codes indicating the number of levels both up to as well as beyond the local level. Only one column is needed for these eight categories. Cases of three or four levels were combined. This seemed justified by the totals indicated by the use of Blaine's cards and the advantage of coding all this information in one column.
1	0	None beyond the local level	
2	1	One beyond the local level	
3	2	Two beyond the local level	
4	3 or 4	Three or four beyond the local level	
		Three or four local levels (where *EA* Column 32 contains code 3 or 4) and:	
5	0	None beyond the local level	
6	1	One beyond the local level	

EA   CODE DEFINITION
Col. Code

32-33   *Jurisdictional Hierarchy* (cont.)

The number of jurisdictional levels of each society is shown by a pair of digits, of which the first indicates the number of levels up to and including the local community and the second beyond the local community. Thus 44 would represent a situation close to the theoretical maximum, e.g. with nuclear family, extended family, clan-barrio, village, parish, district, province, and nation-state; whereas 20 would approximate the theoretical minimum, e.g. nuclear family and nomadic band. The second digit, incidentally, provides a measure of the degree of political complexity, ranging from 0 for stateless societies to 3 or 4 for those organized in large states.

U File $Code$	EA Col.	Code	CODE DEFINITION	EXPLANATION OF CATEGORY REVISION
	32-33		*Jurisdictional Hierarchy* (cont.)	
7		2	Two beyond the local level	
8		3 or 4	Three or four beyond the local level	
9		Blank	No information in either or both *EA* Columns 32 and 33	

EA		CODE DEFINITION
Col. Code		

31   *Mean Size of Local Community*

1   Fewer than 50 persons.
2   From 50 to 99 persons.
3   From 100 to 199 persons.
4   From 200 to 399 persons.
5   From 400 to 1,000 persons.
6   More than 1,000 persons in the absence of any in-
       digenous urban aggregation of more than 5,000.
7   One or more indigenous towns of more than 5,000
       inhabitants but none of more than 50,000.
8   One or more indigenous cities with more than
       50,000 inhabitants.

34   *High Gods*

A   A high god present but otiose or not concerned
       with human affairs.
B   A high god present and active in human affairs
       but not offering positive support to human
       morality.
C   A high god present, active, and specifically sup-
       portive of human morality.
O   A high god absent or not reported in substantial
       descriptions of religious beliefs.

By a high god is meant a spiritual being who is
believed to have created all reality and/or to be its
ultimate governor, even if his sole act was to cre-
ate other spirits who, in turn, created or control
the natural world.

SU File l. Code	EA Col. Code	CODE DEFINITION	EXPLANATION OF CATEGORY REVISION
2	31	*Mean Size of Local Communities*	
1	1	Less than 50	The eight codes were combined into four. The reason for the particular grouping used was the numerical distribution of societies in these categories as discovered by the use of Blaine's cards. Our choice of categories here was based on approximately a normal curve numerical distribution.
2	2,3	50 to 199	
3	4,5	200 to 1,000	
4	6,7, 8	Over 1,000	
0	Blank	No information	
	34	*High Gods*	
1	A	Present, otiose	Categories remain the same.
2	B	Present, active in human affairs, but not in morality	
3	C	Present, active and concerned with human morality	
4	O	Absent, or not reported	
0	Blank	No information	

EA   CODE DEFINITION
Col. Code

19   *Community Organization*

 A Agamous communities without localized clans or any marked tendency toward either local exogamy or local endogamy.

 C Clan-communities, each consisting essentially of a single localized exogamous kin group or clan.

 D Demes, i.e. communities revealing a marked tendency toward local endogamy but not segmented into clan-barrios.

 E Exogamous communities, i.e. those revealing a marked tendency toward local exogamy without having the specific structure of clans.

 S Segmented communities, i.e. those divided into barrios, wards, or hamlets, each of which is essentially a localized kin group or clan, in the absence of any indication of local exogamy.

 T Segmented communities where a marked tendency toward local exogamy is also specifically reported.

SU File l. Code	EA Col. Code	CODE DEFINITION	EXPLANATION OF CATEGORY REVISION
	19	*Community Organization*	
1	A	Agamous communities	These categories remain the same as in the *Atlas*. Lower-case codes are not used.
2	C	Clan-communities	
3	D	Demes	
4	E	Exogamous communities, no clan structure	
5	S	Segmented communities, no local exogamy	
6	T	Segmented communities, with exogamy	
0	Blank	No information	

EA
Col. Code   CODE DEFINITION

14-15   *Family Organization*

E   Large extended families, i.e. corporate aggrega-
     tions of smaller family units occupying a single
     dwelling or a number of adjacent dwellings and
     normally embracing the families of procreation
     of at least two siblings or cousins in each of at
     least two adjacent generations.

F   Small extended families, i.e. those normally em-
     bracing the families of procreation of only one
     individual in the senior generation but of at
     least two individuals in the next generation.
     Families of this type usually dissolve on the
     death of the head.

G   Minimal extended or "stem" families, i.e. those
     consisting of only two related families of pro-
     creation (disregarding polygamous unions), par-
     ticularly of adjacent generations.

M   Independent families with monogamy.

N   Independent families with occasional or limited
     polygyny.

O   Independent polyandrous families.

P   Independent polygynous families, where polygyny
     is general and not reported to be preferentially
     sororal, and where co-wives are not reported to
     occupy separate dwellings or apartments.

SU File Code	EA Col. Code		CODE DEFINITION	EXPLANATION OF CATEGORY REVISION
	14		*Family Organization Independent Family*	
1		M	Monogamy	The data contained in *EA* Columns 14 and 15 cover both the family organization structure and the form of marriage. This information is organized into four separate columns in the OSU File. In this way, it is possible to assign one column for each family structure (i.e. independent, small extended, large extended, and stem). Within each column the form of marriage (e.g. monogamy, polygny, etc.) is indicated. Totals can then easily be gotten, to indicate family structure and form of marriage within each structure. As a further change, we combined all forms of polygny into one code.
2		N	Monogamy, with occasional polygyny	
3		O	Polyandry	
4		P,Q, R,S	Polygny	
5		Blank	No information	
	15		*Large Extended Family* (where *EA* Column 15 contains code E)	
1		m	Monogamy	
2		n	Monogamy, with occasional polygyny	
3		o	Polyandry	
4		p,q, r,s	Polygny	

EA
Col. Code
                                    CODE DEFINITION

14-15   *Family Organization* (cont.)

        Q   Independent polygynous families, where polygyny
                is general and not specified as preferentially so-
                roral, and where co-wives typically occupy sep-
                arate dwellings or apartments.

        R   Independent polygynous families, where polygyny
                is common and preferentially sororal, and where
                co-wives are not reported to occupy separate
                dwellings.

        S   Independent polygynous families, where polygyny
                is common and preferentially sororal, and
                where co-wives normally occupy separate dwell-
                ings.

                (Lower-case letters from *m* to *s*, following E, F
                or G, suggest the marital composition of the com-
                ponent familial units in extended families, e.g.
                Gm for stem families with monogamy.)

SU File . Code	EA Col. Code	CODE DEFINITION	EXPLANATION OF CATEGORY REVISION
	15	*Large Extended Family* (cont.)	
5	Blank	No information, Column 15	
	15	*Small Extended Family* (where *EA* Column 14 contains code F)	
1	m	Monogamy	
2	n	Monogamy, with occasional polygyny	
3	o	Polyandry	
4	p,q, r,s	Polygyny	
5	Blank	No information, Column 15	
	15	*Stem Family* (where *EA* Column 14 contains code G)	
1	m	Monogamy	
2	n	Monogamy, with occasional polygyny	
3	o	Polyandry	
4	p,q, r,s	Polygyny	
5	Blank	No information, Column 15	

EA
Col. Code   CODE DEFINITION

16-18   *Profile of Marital Residence*
     A   Avunculocal, i.e. normal residence with or near
          the maternal uncle or other male matrilineal
          kinsmen of the husband.
     B   Ambilocal, i.e. residence established optionally
          with or near the parents of either the husband or
          the wife, depending upon circumstances or per-
          sonal choice, where neither alternative exceeds
          the other in actual frequency by a ratio greater
          than two to one. If the differential frequency
          is greater than this, the symbols *Uv* or *Vu* are
          used to denote, respectively, a marked prepon-
          derance of uxorilocal or virilocal practice.
     C   Optionally uxorilocal or avunculocal. This may
          be the case in a uxorilocal society where many
          men marry a MoBrDa and thus, in fact, live
          avunculocally.
     D   Optionally patrilocal (or virilocal) or avunculocal.
     M   Matrilocal, i.e. normal residence with or near the
          female matrilineal kinsmen of the wife. Cf. *U*
          Uxorilocal.
     N   Neolocal, i.e. normal residence apart from the rel-
          atives of both spouses or at a place not deter-
          mined by the kin ties of either.
     O   Nonestablishment of a common household, i.e.
          where both spouses remain in their natal house-
          holds, sometimes called "duolocal" or "nato-
          local" residence.
     P   Patrilocal, i.e. normal residence with or near the
          male patrilineal kinsmen of the husband. Cf. *V*
          Virilocal.

U File Code	EA Col. Code	CODE DEFINITION	EXPLANATION OF CATEGORY REVISION
	17	*Profile of Marital Residence*	
1	O	Nonestablishment of a common household	The ten categories of the *Atlas* have been combined into eight. Codes B, C, and D were combined into one group because all these residence patterns involve an option. Also, only five cases of C or D were found in the 603 societies for which data were available on Blaine's cards.
2	N	Neolocal	
3	P	Patrilocal	
4	V	Virilocal	
5	M	Matrilocal	
6	U	Uxorilocal	
7	A	Avunculocal	
8	B,C, D	Optional—Ambilocal	
0	Blank	No information	

EA
Col. Code   CODE DEFINITION

16-18   *Profile of Marital Residence* (cont.)

U   Uxorilocal. Equivalent to "matrilocal" but con-
          fined to instances where the wife's matrikin are
          not aggregated in matrilocal and matrilineal kin
          groups.

V   Virilocal. Equivalent to "patrilocal" but confined
          to instances where the husband's patrikin are
          not aggregated in patrilocal and patrilineal kin
          groups.

          (Lower-case letters following a capital indicate
          culturally patterned alternatives to, or numerically
          significant deviations from, the prevailing profile.)
          (Lower-case letters preceding a capital indicate
          the existence of a different rule or profile for the
          first year or so of marriage, e.g. *uP* for initial
          uxorilocal residence followed by permanent patri-
          local residence.)

20-21   *Patrilineal Kin Groups and Exogamy*

          (A capital letter indicates the largest type of kin
          groups reported for the particular society. A lower-
          case letter following a capital indicates the largest
          kin group characterized by exogamy, if it is dif-
          ferent.)

E   Patrilineal exogamy, i.e. extension of incest taboos
          to known patrilineal kinsmen in the absence of
          true patrilineal kin groups, provided such ex-
          tension does not apply generally to bilateral
          kinsmen of equal remoteness.

U File Code	EA Col. Code		CODE DEFINITION	EXPLANATION OF CATEGORY REVISION

KIN GROUPS

1	20	E,L, M,P, or S	Patrilineal (where *EA* Column 22 contains O or blank)	We have recorded all Kin Groups codes in one column in OSU File. In coding these, we collapsed all the categories within each of the kin groups.
2	22	E,L, M,P, or S	Matrilineal (where *EA* Column 20 contains O or blank)	
3	20 &22	E,L, M,P, or S	Double Descent	Some societies have been coded by the *Atlas* for both Matrilineal and Patrilineal Kin Groups.
4	24	A,B, K,Q, R,S	Cognatic	We have identified these societies and put into a group called Double Descent.
0	20, 22, &24	Blank	No information	

Our coding indicates four groups: Patrilineal, Matrilineal, Double Descent, and Cognatic Kin Groups.

Lower-case codes are not used.

EA	CODE DEFINITION
Col. Code	

20-21   *Patrilineal Kin Groups and Exogamy* (cont.)

L   Lineages of modest size, i.e. patrilineal kin groups whose core membership is normally confined to a single community or a part thereof.

M   Moieties, i.e. maximal lineages when there are only two such in the society.

O   Absence of any patrilineal kin groups and also of patrilineal exogamy.

P   Phratries, i.e. maximal lineages when there are more than two and when sibs are also present. Segmentary lineage systems in which segment of a lower order or magnitude are equivalent to sibs will also be designated by *P*.

S   Sibs ("clans" in British usage), i.e. lineages whose core membership normally comprises resident of more than one community.

22-23   *Matrilineal Kin Groups and Exogamy*
Codes and definitions are identical to those under *Patrilineal Kin Groups and Exogamy*, except that the word "Matrilineal" must be substituted for "Patrilineal" in each case.

EA
Col. Code   CODE DEFINITION

24   *Cognatic Kin Groups*
    A   Ambilineal descent as inferred from the presence
            of ambilocal extended families, true ramages
            being absent or unreported.
    B   Bilateral descent as inferred from the absence of
            reported ambilineal, matrilineal, or patrilineal
            kin groups, kindreds being absent or unreported.
    K   Kindreds, i.e. Ego-oriented bilateral kin groups,
            specifically reported.
    O   Absence of cognatic kin groups as inferred from
            the presence of unilineal descent.
    Q   Quasi-lineages, i.e. cognatic groups approximat-
            ing the structure of lineages but based on filia-
            tion rather than on unilineal or ambilineal de-
            scent.
    R   Ramages, i.e. ancestor-oriented ambilineal kin
            groups comparable to lineages under patrilineal
            or matrilineal descent, specifically reported, if
            they are agamous, endogamous, or not specifi-
            cally stated to be exogamous.
    S   Exogamous ramages specifically reported.
            (When both kindreds and ramages are reported
            for the same society, they are indicated by a capital
            letter followed by a lower-case letter, the former
            designating the group of the greater functional
            importance.)

EA
Col. Code   CODE DEFINITION

12-13   *Mode of Marriage*
    B   Bride-price or bridewealth, i.e. transfer of a sub-
             stantial consideration in the form of livestock,
             goods, or money from the groom or his relatives
             to the kinsmen of the bride.
    D   Dowry, i.e. transfer of a substantial amount of
             property from the bride's relatives to the bride,
             the groom, or the kinsmen of the latter.
    G   Gift exchange, i.e. reciprocal exchange of gifts of
             substantial value between the relatives of the
             bride and groom, or a continuing exchange of
             goods and service in approximately equal
             amounts between the groom or his kinsmen and
             the bride's relatives. *Gb* and *Gd* indicate unequal
             exchanges which tend to approach, respectively,
             a bride-price or a dowry.
    O   Absence of any significant consideration, or bridal
             gifts only.
    S   Bride service, i.e. a substantial material considera-
             tion in which the principal element consists of
             labor or other service rendered by the groom to
             the bride's kinsmen.
    T   Token bride-price, i.e. a small or symbolic pay-
             ment only.
    X   Exchange, i.e. transfer of a sister or other female
             relative of the groom in exchange for the bride.

SU File Code	EA Col. Code	CODE DEFINITION	EXPLANATION OF CATEGORY REVISION
		Mode of Marriage	
		12-13	
1	B or S	Bride-price, bride service	The seven categories of the *Atlas* have been combined into four categories. Bride-price and bride service are combined, because in both cases the husband's kin is giving to the bride's kin a substantial consideration.
2	D	Dowry	
3	G or X	Gift exchange, exchange of persons	
4	T or O	Token bride-price or absence of any significant consideration	
5	Blank	No information	

EA *Col. Code*	CODE DEFINITION

25-26   *Cousin Marriage*

C   Duolateral cross-cousin marriage, i.e. marriage allowed with either cross cousin but forbidden with a parallel cousin. A lower-case letter is appended to indicate preferential, as opposed to merely permitted unions, i.e. Cc, Cm, or Cp, respectively, for a symmetrical, matrilateral, or patrilateral preference.

D   Duolateral marriage with paternal cousins only. Da or Dp for a preference for FaBrDa or FaSiDa respectively.

E   Duolateral marriage with maternal cousins only. Em for a preference for MoBrDa.

F   Duolateral marraige with an uncle's daughter only. Fa or Fm for a preference for FaBrDa or MoBrDa respectively.

G   Duolateral marriage with an aunt's daughter only. Gp for a preference for FaSiDa.

M   Matrilateral cross-cousin marriage, i.e. unilateral marriage with a MoBrDa only. Mm if preferred rather than merely permitted.

N   Nonlateral marriage, i.e. unions forbidden with any first or second cousin.

O   Nonlateral marriage when evidence is available only for first cousins, the rule or practice regarding second cousins being unreported.

P   Patrilateral cross-cousin marriage, i.e. unilateral marriage with a FaSiDa only. Pp if preferred rather than merely permitted.

OSU File Code	EA Col. Code	CODE DEFINITION	EXPLANATION OF CATEGORY REVISION
	25	*Cousin Marriage*	
1	N,O, R,S	Nonlateral	The fourteen categories of the *Atlas* have been combined into seven. Combinations of codes are based on frequencies obtained from Blaine's cards. Although *P* is rare (seven cases) and *U* is absent in Blaine's cards, these codes were kept for future possible uses, because of their theoretical interest. (All lower-case letters have been omitted.)
2	C,D, E,F, G	Duolateral	
3	Q	Quadrilateral	
4	M	Matrilateral	
5	T	Trilateral	
6	P	Patrilateral	
7	U	Unilateral	
0	Blank	No information	

EA	CODE DEFINITION
Col. Code	

25-26   *Cousin Marriage* (cont.)

Q   Quadrilateral marriage, i.e. marriage allowed with any first cousin. Qa for the Arabic or Islamic variant in which the FaBrDa is the preferred mate. Qc, Qm, and Qp for other preferences.

R   Nonlateral marriage in which all first cousins and some but not all second cousins are forbidden as spouses. Rr for the type of preferential marriage with particular second cross cousins only, notably MoMoBrDaDa or FaMoBrSiDa, often characteristic of societies with subsection systems.

S   Nonlateral marriage in which unions are forbidden with any first cousin but are permitted with any second cousin (or at least any who is not a lineage mate). Ss if second cousin is preferred rather than merely permitted.

T   Trilateral marriage, i.e. marriage allowed with any first cousin except an ortho-cousin or lineage mate. Tc, Tm, and Tp, respectively, for preferences for a bilateral, matrilateral, or patrilateral cross cousin.

U   Unilateral marriage with a particular parallel cousin only. Ua for a preference for FaBrDa.

(Two positions will be required for punch-card entries. In the one registering capital letters, the unusual forms of duolateral marriage—D,E,F, and G—will be classed together as D. In the second, registering preferential or prescriptive unions only, the lower-case letters [a, c, m, p, r, and s] should be distinguished and all other instances grouped under a separate category to indicate the absence of preferential rules.)

EA *Col. Code*		CODE DEFINITION

78

Norms of Premarital Sex Behavior

The following symbols define the standards of sex behavior prevailing for unmarried females:

A   Premarital sex relations allowed and not sanctioned unless pregnancy results.

E   Early marriage of females, i.e. at or before puberty, precluding the possibility of premarital sex relations as defined.

F   Premarital sex relations freely permitted and no sanctioned even if pregnancy results.

P   Premarital sex relations prohibited but weakly sanctioned and not infrequent in fact.

T   Trial marriage; monogamous premarital sex relations permitted with the expectation of marriage if pregnancy results, promiscuous relation being prohibited and sanctioned.

V   Insistence on virginity; premarital sex relations prohibited, strongly sanctioned, and in fact rare.

36

Postpartum Sex Taboo

0   No taboo, especially where the husband is expected to have intercourse with his wife as soon a possible after childbirth for the alleged benefit of the child.

1   Short postpartum taboo, lasting not more than one month.

2   Duration of from more than one month to si months.

3   Duration of from more than six months to one year.

4   Duration of from more than one year to two years.

5   Duration of more than two years.

SU File Code	EA Col. Code	CODE DEFINITION	EXPLANATION OF CATEGORY REVISION
		78 *Norms of Premarital Sex Behavior*	
1	A,F,P, or T	Little restriction	These six codes were combined into two. The codes A, F, P, or T were combined and indicate situations where few restrictions exist.
2	E or V	Early marriage of females; insistence on virginity	
0	Blank	No information	The codes E and V indicate a concern for virginity and early marriage of females, which are situations of much greater restriction of activity.
		36 *Postpartum Sex Taboo*	
1	1 or 0	No taboo; less than one month	The five categories were reduced to three. This was based in part on the number of cases falling into each category, as indicated by totals from Blaine's cards.
2	2 or 3	Between one month and one year	
3	4 or 5	More than one year	
0	Blank	No information	

| *EA* | CODE DEFINITION |
| *Col. Code* | |

38   *Segregation of Adolescent Boys*

A   Absence of segregation, adolescent boys residing and sleeping in the same dwelling as their mothers and sisters.

P   Partial segregation, adolescent boys residing or eating with their natal families but sleeping apart from them, e.g. in a special hut or in a cattle shed.

R   Complete segregation, in which adolescent boys go to live as individuals with relatives outside the nuclear family, e.g. with grandparents or with a maternal or paternal uncle.

S   Complete segregation, in which adolescent boys go to live as individuals with nonrelatives, e.g. as retainers to a chief or as apprentices to specialists.

T   Complete segregation, in which adolescent boys reside with a group of their own peers, e.g. in bachelor dormitories, military regiments, or age-villages.

U File Code	EA Col. Code	CODE DEFINITION	EXPLANATION OF CATEGORY REVISION
	38	*Segregation of Adolescent Boys*	
1	A	Absence of segregation	The five *Atlas* codes were combined into three, showing complete or partial segregation or absence of this practice.
2	P	Partial segregation	
3	R,S, or T	Complete segregation	
0	Blank	No information	

EA		CODE DEFINITION
Col.	*Code*	

37   *Male Genital Mutilations*

0   Absent or not generally practiced.

1   Performed shortly after birth, i.e. within the first two months.

2   Performed during infancy, i.e. from two month to two years of age.

3   Performed during early childhood, i.e. from two to five years of age.

4   Performed during late childhood, i.e. from six to ten years of age.

5   Performed during adolescence, i.e. from eleven to fifteen years of age.

6   Performed during early adulthood, i.e. from sixteen to twenty-five years of age.

7   Performed during maturity, i.e. from twenty-five to fifty years of age.

8   Performed in old age, i.e. after fifty years of age.

9   Circumcision customary, but the normal age unspecified or unclear.

J File *Code*	*EA* *Col.* *Code*	CODE DEFINITION	EXPLANATION OF CATEGORY REVISION
	37	*Male Genital Muti-* *lations*	
1	0	Absent	The nine codes were reduced to five.
2	1,2, 3, or 4	Ten years and younger	Categories and codes were chosen to show practices before, dur-
3	5	Eleven to fifteen years	ing, and after ado- lescence.
4	6,7, or 8	Sixteen years and over	
5	9	Age unspecified	
0	Blank	No information	

EA
Col. Code   CODE DEFINITION

35   *Types of Games*
    A   Games of physical skill only, whether or not they
                may also involve incidental elements of chance
                or strategy, e.g. foot racing, wrestling, the
                hoop-and-pole game.
    B   Games of chance only, with no significant ele-
                ment of either physical skill or strategy in-
                volved, e.g. dice games.
    C   Games of physical skill and of chance both pres-
                ent.
    O   No games of any of the three types.
    P   Games of strategy only, involving no significant
                element of physical skill, e.g. chess, go, poker.
                Whether or not an element of chance is also in-
                volved is considered irrelevant.
    Q   Games of physical skill and of strategy present,
                but not games of chance.
    R   Games of chance and of strategy present, but not
                games of physical skill.
    S   Games of all three types present.

SU File l. Code	EA Col. Code	CODE DEFINITION	EXPLANATION OF CATEGORY REVISION
	35	*Types of Games*	
1	A	Physical skill	The eight categories were reduced to five. The codes included in the "all other" category seemed justified by the few cases in these groups evidenced by the totals from Blaine's cards. Other codes remained the same.
2	C	Physical skill and chance	
3	Q	Physical skill and strategy	
4	S	Skill, chance, and strategy	
5	B,O, P, or R	All others	
0	Blank	No information	
3-60		*Blank columns for research use*	
1-64		*Date of observation of society*	The information of Columns 61-80 was derived from the cluster listing in the *Atlas,* but not supplied in its tables.
5-73		*Estimated population of society*	
4-77		*Date of population estimate, if different from date of observation*	
8-80		*Cluster number*	

APPENDIX II

The Ohio State University
Punched Card File
of Ethnographic Data:

Listing of Societies by Cluster

Appendix II

The Ohio State University Punched Card File of Ethnographic Data, which served as the basis for all tabulations, is listed in detail in the following pages.

The 863 societies in this listing are arranged according to the major ethnographic region to which they belong. Within each region the societies are grouped into clusters, as developed by Murdock (1967a, 1967b). The number of societies per cluster ranges from one to nine, the majority of clusters, however, have only one society. Clusters with more than one society generally contain societies from the same major region. Only 5 of the 412 clusters contain societies from a neighboring region. These clusters are:

Cluster 51 — Senegal (Africa) includes Wolof (Circum-Mediterranean).

Cluster 52 — Sedentary Fulani (Africa) includes Tukulor (Circum-Mediterranean).

Cluster 96 — Nubians (Circum-Mediterranean) includes Nyima (Africa), Dilling (Africa).

Cluster 149 — Mongols (East Eurasia) includes Kalmyk (Circum-Mediterranean).

Cluster 207 — Sea Gypsies (East Eurasia) includes Tawi-Tawi Badjaw (Insular Pacific).

The listing of the societies by cluster requires some further comment. Clusters were developed by Murdock in two presentations (1966, 1967a, 1967b). In the second of these, all of the societies of the *Atlas* are grouped into 412 clusters. The total number of relatively independent clusters in the world is estimated at "approximately 430," a number which "would complete the identification and 'stratification' of the known cultural universe."

The concept of clusters is best understood by noting that:

> The fundamental criterion for the establishment of clusters is the assumption that at least 1,000 years of separation and divergent evolution are necessary before two societies derived from a common ancestor are likely to develop sufficient differences to be treated as independent cases for comparative purposes [Murdock 1967a: 112].

Historical, ethnographic and linguistic evidence was utilized to estimate time depth. Societies of common origin but not separated for 1,000 years are generally assigned to the same cluster. In a few cases, neighboring societies without common origins are assigned to the same cluster because of cultural similarities developed over time. The clusters, then, are to be viewed as genetic and historical rather than typological groupings. Furthermore, we are told, for purposes of sampling that the "members of a cluster are in a sense interchangeable" (Murdock 1967a: 113).

Presentation of the societies of the *Ethnographic Atlas* grouped into clusters makes it possible for the reader to see by inspection the clusters that contain more than one specimen society, how great the differences between these societies are, and which variables they affect.

Since the primary aim in the classification of societies into clusters was to present a basis for cross-cultural sampling, a study of cluster homogeneity or heterogeneity and of similarities between clusters may take us a step further in an understanding of the interrelationship between various dimensions of societies, and may provide some leads for the study of structural changes as well. Pointing to intracluster heterogeneity, Köbben (1967) has questioned Murdock's argument in favor of selecting no more than one component society of a cluster in the development of a sample for cross-cultural analysis. Greenbaum (1970) discovered no statistically significant differences between samples in which one society per cluster was selected (following Murdock's instructions in the 1967 Summary) and samples selecting societies on a completely random basis disregarding cluster designation. Her work further raised questions over the claimed interchangeability of societies within clusters.

It is hoped that the following listing represents a contribution to this discussion.

Listing of the OSU File Cards
in Cluster Number Sequence

COLS 1 - 6	COLS 7-11	COLS 12 - 23	COLS 24 - 34	COLS 35 - 47	COLS 61-64	COLS 65 - 73	COLS 74 - 80

SUB SAHARAN AFRICA

001	PYGMIES						
100202	MBUTI	321114256631	99--1151141	2---843113330	1930	10000	001
002	BUSHMEN						
100001	KUNG	411114256639	99--1145124	--2-841122211	1950	3500	1953002
100636	NARON	321114256639	99--1141114	2---444103010	1910	550	002
003	HOTTENTOT						
100102	NAMA	121313251233	59--1342242	2---313212214	1840	24000	1946003
004	NGUNI						
110003	SWAZI	111131221239	361-2548042	-4--311200230	1880	180000	1946004
110401	NDEBE	111231121239	362-4518411	4---311100310	1870	300000	1948004
110402	PONDO	111331141233	76--2347004	--4-311100000		260000	1936004
110404	ZULU	111231121939	361-2548002	--4-311100310	1830	250000	1921004
120351	NGONI	111132221939	361-4604241	4---444200310	1940	85000	1950004
005	SOTHO						
110204	VENDA	111131241239	362-4647325	-4--331213344	1900	150000	1930005
110303	SOTHO	11231141239	361-2548341	4---311300010	1860	900000	1953005
110405	TSWAN	111231121939	362-4547435	4---341311340	1880	580000	1946005
006	SHONA-THONGA						
110104	THONG	111231121233	361-4543002	-4--311113334	1920	1000000	006
110406	LOVED	111231141239	351-2507312	4---311212130	1930	40000	006
110408	LENGE	111132225230	36--2046002	--4-311100000	1930		006
110410	SHONA	111132221233	35--2043232	4---311100030	1920	700000	1931006
007	ILA-TONGA						
120004	ILA	111231121233	361-3436311	--4-431613213	1920	22000	1957007
120744	PTONG	111131221233	361-2235321	--4-821213210	1940	90000	1948007
008	BAROTSELAND						
110103	LOZI	111122241233	321-3644211	4---444100010	1890	67000	1934008
009	SOUTHWESTERN BANTU						
110002	HERER	121312251239	591-1445004	--4-431200250	1900	100000	1930009
110302	NYANE	111221121931	31--2637002	--4-721200030	1920	40000	1920009
110411	AMBO	111231121233	361-2617000	4---421102233	1910	60000	1948009
010	WESTERN ANGOLA						
110203	MBUND	111132221233	361-4647312	4---331200213	1930	1200000	1940010
011	LOWER CONGO						
120005	PENDE	111131225092	06--4636002	4---724600000	1920	27000	1955011
120305	YOMBE	111132225033	061-4636302	4---721100350	1930	170000	1933011
120728	KONGO	111132225133	061-4636002	2---721210330	1900		011
120731	SUKU	111132225031	061-4638211	4---421203230	1910	80000	1949011
120732	SUNDI	111132225133	361-4036202	--4-721000350	1910	65000	1953011
012	KASAI						
120106	KUBA	111132225933	961-5617215	--2-721102224	1910	73000	1947012
120735	BUNDA	111131225031	06--2633002	4---721200300	1910		012
120736	DZING	111132225032	36--5036204	4---721100300	1930		012
120737	LELE	111131225232	061-4636241	4---721100300	1950	10000	1947012
120739	SONGO	111132225130	06--4236004	4---721500300	1930		012
013	LUNDA						
120206	NDEMB	111132225933	061-5033102	4---724200300	1930	63000	013
120668	LUVAL	112132225031	072-4236012	--4-724210330	1930	90000	1940013
120698	CHOKW	121132225033	061-4633002	2---724200300	1920	600000	1940013
120742	LUIMB	112213221033	021-4036004	4---821200000	1930	40000	1950013

COLS 1-6	COLS 7-11	COLS 12-23	COLS 24-34	COLS 35-47	COLS 61-64	COLS 65-73	COLS 74-80
014	BEMBA-LAMBA						
120105	BEMBA	111132225233	061-5637221	4---821222310	1900	150000	1951014
120205	LAMBA	111132226933	951-4233011	2---821201013	1920	70000	014
120747	LALA	111132225033	36--4632212	2---721410010	1940	60000	1950014
120748	LUAPU	112132225033	061-4637321	2---721200030	1940	100000	014
120750	TUMBU	111131225030	061-4647024	4---311203010	1920	115000	1945014
015	MARAVI						
120637	CHEWA	111132221233	361-4237245	4---721222210	1920	750000	1955015
120703	LTONG	112123225003	021-2235215	2---721200000	1950	50000	1953015
120752	NYANJ	111132225033	061-2236001	4---521200010	1910	575000	1945015
016	YAO-MAKONDE						
120304	YAO	111132226933	061-2236245	-2--524213023	1920	360000	1945016
017	NGONDE						
130208	NYAKY	11131241933	371-4223211	4---211120315	1930	163000	1931017
130758	NGOND	11131241033	371-4613044	4---211100310	1920	60000	1945017
018	RUKWA						
130757	IWA	11141225030	351-4643212	4---311200010	1900	12000	1953018
130759	SAFWA	11131221230	35--4042004	4---311000300	1920	45000	1950018
130761	FIPA	112132221033	361-4623210	4---311100310	1910	85000	1957018
130763	PIMBW	111132225033	36--4623010	4---311100010	1930	11000	1957018
019	NYAMWEZI						
130762	NYAMW	111132225230	36--4603204	2---441100310	1920		019
130764	SUKUM	11231141039	361-2617001	4---441110310	1950	1000000	1948019
020	HATSA						
100726	HATSA	331114256679	99--1111100	2---441000010	1910	600	020
021	RIFT						
100301	SANDA	111132221232	36--2102012	2---311400020	1920	23000	1948021
130766	GOGO	11231121039	361-2646302	--4-311200030	1910	100000	1910021
130768	TURU	11331141009	761-2155002	--4-311100250	1910	145000	1949021
022	RUFIJI						
130307	HEHE	11231141939	361-2607002	--4-311203210	1910	85000	1930022
130638	BENA	11231141233	361-4613031	4---211203310	1930	16000	1931022
023	LUGURU-ZIGULA						
130704	LUGUR	111141225033	07--2245005	2---521203000	1930	200000	1960023
024	SWAHILI						
130006	BAJUN	112123221933	31--4241001	1---211300130	1950	2000	1950024
130771	HADIM	11131221031	353-4624030	4---341300030	1930	100000	1924024
025	NYIKA						
130772	DIGO	111132225030	361-4042035	4---331100050	1890	112000	1948025
130774	GIRIA	11131221030	361-4258044	-4--311100030	1900	120000	1948025
130775	POKOM	112132246033	961-4252001	2---311100330	1900	20000	1948025
026	KENYA HIGHLANDS						
130107	CHAGG	11231141939	151-2542342	4---311112334	1910	235000	1948026
130108	KIKUY	11231141939	362-4335322	4---311102343	1930	1000000	1948026
130629	SHAMB	11231141032	361-4647202	4---311100320	1910	220000	1948026
130777	MERU	11231121039	361-2255002	4---311100330	1940	255000	1948026
027	EAST NYANZA						
130352	GISU	11131221930	361-2446012	4---311110240	1900	250000	027
130781	SONJO	11141245939	152-4521305	2---311120030	1950	4500	1957027
130783	VUGUS	11231121033	361-2005302	2---311110030	1930	50000	1937027
028	EAST LACUSTRINE BANTU						
130007	NYORO	11131241933	365-2644315	4---311100113	1900	110000	1957028
130306	GANDA	11131241933	364-4614414	4---211113213	1880	800000	1948028
130784	HAYA	11131141033	361-2643314	4---311100010	1900	325000	1957028
130788	SOGA	11131141033	364-2613001	4---311100310	1950	425000	1948028
029	WEST LACUSTRINE BANTU						
130669	CHIGA	11131221933	36--2205002	-4--311400110	1930	100000	1940029
130786	KONJO	112132225003	371-2041012	4---311000010	1920	375000	1959029
130787	NYANK	11231121030	361-2604210	4---311100010	1920	520000	1959029
140309	RUNDI	11231141933	353-2848015	4---314222113	1910	2000000	029
140641	RUAND	11231141130	353-2848012	4---311220113	1910	2130000	1952029
140793	HA	11231141030	362-2647012	--4-311200210	1950	200000	1948029
140794	HUNDE	11231141033	351-4803002	4---311000010	1940		029
030	LUBA						
140210	LUBA	111123225233	021-4648001	4---311000010	1930		030
140796	REGA	111132225233	06--4142001	4---311120050	1900		030
031	MONGO						
140110	NKUND	111132225233	961-2247012	-4--331111220	1930	150000	1940031
140801	KUTSH	111132225030	06--4246001	--4-311100050	1900		031

COLS 1 - 6	COLS 7-11	COLS 12 - 23	COLS 24 - 34	COLS 35 - 47	COLS 61-64	COLS 65 - 73	COLS 74 - 80

```
032    RIVERAIN CONGO
140670 SONGO  113114225037 02--4242002 4---311100350 1900      100000      032
140807 NGALA  112123225031 02--4406311 -4--311000022 1900      125000 1950032
140808 POTO   113114225337 021-4246002 -4--311110050 1900              032
033    BABWA-BIRA
140008 AVBA   111132225033 361-2155242 4---313110110 1950       18000 1948033
140308 BABWA  111132226032 06--2207002 --4-311000210 1910       16000 1924033
034    NGOMBE
140817 NDOKO  111141226032 06--4235004 -4--821000000 1920              034
140818 NGOMB  111132226231 261-4226245 -4--311112125 1920              034
035    FANG-DZEM
140109 FANG   111132225233 361-4345212 --4-311113131 1910      850000 1950035
140820 KOTA   111132225032 061-4245005 2---311120230 1940              035
036    BIAFRA COAST
140009 KPE    111231121032 361-4455215 4---331103020 1950       38000 1953036
140699 DUALA  112132225033 061-4447012 4---311000121 1940       40000 1947036
037    MIDDLE CAMEROON
140827 BAFIA  111131225003 061-2245002 4---311010330 1930       12000 1949037
140830 BANEN  111131225031 161-2241012 4---313000030 1940       25000 1949037
038    CAMEROON HIGHLANDS
140209 BAMIL  111141226939 061-2647005 4---311100210 1910      455000 1951038
140640 FUT    111141225039 06--4646025 --4-311100000 1950       34000 1953038
140829 BAMUM  111131225030 161-4648025 --4-311020050 1920       80000 1951038
140834 NDOB   111131225032 061-4006005 --4-311000000 1950       44000 1953038
140835 NSAW   111141225030 06--4607325 --4-311100000 1950       60000 1953038
039    CROSS RIVER
150112 YAKO   111131221139 35--4235445 --4-331203010 1930       20000      039
040    COASTAL NIGERIA
150919 EFIK   112132221033 35--4426015 -4--311102020 1950       30000 1945040
150920 IBIBI  111132221033 36--2446315 -4--311100120 1910     1000000      040
150922 ITSEK  113114225037 001-4616015 4---314110020 1940       33000 1952040
041    IBO-EDO
150643 IBO    111141221033 061-2456315 -4--311100120 1930     3500000 1950041
150923 AFIKP  111132241003 061-4456445 --4-331522220 1950              041
150924 EDO    111131225230 053-4648415 ---4311100020 1900      200000 1952041
150925 ISOKO  112132225333 061-4416015 -4--311103120 1930      435000 1952041
042    NUPE-IDOMA
150311 NUPE   111131225230 371-2817335 -4--311223220 1930      360000 1955042
150672 IGBIR  111132221033 061-4606015 -4--311100120 1920      150000 1952042
150928 GBARI  111131245030 072-4046025 -4--311122010 1910      200000 1960042
043    YORUBA
150212 YORUB  111141225290 271-4848415 -4--311113120 1950      220000 1931043
150932 EGBA   111141225030 271-4607415 -4--311100050 1920      500000      043
150933 EKITI  111131221000 071-4607415 -4--311103150 1950      220000      043
044    EWE-FON
150010 FON    111132225933 163-4648445 4---311522244 1890      250000      044
150936 EWE    111132225033 051-4627015 -4--311210020 1900      700000 1948044
045    AKAN
150111 ASHAN  111132225933 052-4627411 --4-731221313 1900      800000 1948045
150642 BAULE  111132225031 071-4236005 -4--724210010 1900      385000 1950045
150942 FANTI  111132225033 051-4626011 --4-831200010 1900      200000 1950045
150943 GA     112123225033 03--4045045 --4-111300020 1930              045
046    KRU
150310 BETE   111131225931 06--4115302 --4-311100000 1950      150000 1956046
150949 SAPO   111132221033 061-4246202 4---311113051 1940              046
047    SOUTHERN MANDE
150951 GAGU   121132225332 06--4145305 --4-311000010 1920       13000 1950047
150952 GURO   111132221032 07--4246305 -4--311010010 1920       13000 1950047
150956 NGERE  111131221031 061-4046315 4---311113034 1930       70000 1950047
048    MENDE-TEMNE
150011 KISSI  111141221933 35--4206206 --4-311400230 1950      200000 1954048
150211 MENDE  111131225332 051-4646315 --4-311403334 1930      580000 1931048
150644 TOMA   111132221033 061-4246312 4---311500334 1920      150000 1950048
150700 SHERB  111132221033 061-4007010 --4-421100050 1930      100000 1948048
150705 KPELL  111132221332 061-4426315 --4-311410334 1920      175000 1950048
150954 GBAND  111131221030 161-4246315 4---311110034 1930       25000 1930048
150957 TEMNE  111131221032 053-4007012 --4-311103030 1910      525000 1948048
```

```
COLS     COLS      COLS        COLS         COLS       COLS    COLS     COLS
1 - 6    7-11      12 - 23     24 - 34      35 - 47    61-64   65 - 73  74 - 80


049     GUINEA
160961  BANYU   111131224332  27--2145000  --4-311510230  1930    7500 1950049
160963  BIJOG   111132221331  07--4236000  2---524110010  1930   20000 1945049
130964  DIOLA   112122221031  32--4146000  -4--311110030  1930   50000 1950049
050     TENDA
160313  CONIA   111132221239  151-4136211  2---721513320  1910   11000 1945050
160966  BASSA   111131221233  351-4132011  2---321013220  1910    7600 1945050
051     SENEGAL
160967  SERER   111132221031  173-2647001  -4--331210200  1920  300000 1950051
210021  WOLOF   11231121233   374-4847432  --4-331213124  1950  850000     051
052     SEDENTARY FULANI
160214  FUTAJ   111331121999  571-4607035  4---311310230  1890  720000 1940052
211081  TUKUL   11231121033   373-4616030  -4--311310020  1930  275000 1950052
053     NUCLEAR MANDE
160012  BAMBA   111132241233  173-4646445  -4--311203030  1920 1000000 1954053
160645  MALIN   111132221233  373-4646001  -4--311200230  1930  830000 1950053
160970  SONIN   111131221000  072-4607031  --4-311320030  1900  360000 1950053
160971  SUSU    111131221000  372-4006005  -4--311200050  1930  300000 1950053
054     MARKA
160972  DIULA   111131225039  071-4406035  -4--311300220  1910  160000 1950054
055     NIGER FISHERMEN
160312  BOZO    113124246997  93--3206030  -4--311300330  1930   29000 1942055
056     HABE
160113  DOGON   111131241139  372-4446206  -2--311100030  1930  225000 1957056
160975  BOBO    111131225232  071-2245305  -4--311000030  1910  240000 1952056
057     SENUFO
160976  MINIA   111131225030  072-4247005  -4--311020030  1910  150000 1942057
160977  SENUF   111131245233  072-4206005  -4--311210020  1900  540000 1948057
058     LOBI
160213  BIRIF   111132221231  37--2205212  -4--331203110  1930   85000     058
160674  LOBI    111132221231  37--2205201  4---421200010  1910  100000     058
059     GRUSI
160014  TALLE   111131241233  371-2415342  --4-331113112  1930   35000 1931059
160675  NANKA   111131221033  37--2245012  --4-331103110  1910   70000 1948059
160706  KASEN   111131221000  071-4046002  --4-311103110  1910   40000 1948059
160986  KUSAS   11231141000   071-2045012  -4--331103010  1920   93000 1948059
060     MOLE
160013  YATEN   111131241239  353-2807415  -4--311102325  1950  400000 1950060
160992  MOSSI   111131221233  351-2648415  4---311100024  1900 1300000 1950060
061     BORGU-MANGO
160673  KONKO   111132221233  351-2255012  4---311503110  1940   60000 1948061
160993  BASAR   111131241033  072-4216002  -4--311013010  1890   40000 1950061
160994  KABRE   111131241030  061-2215015  4---311100210  1930  160000 1950061
062     MIDDLE NIGER
170998  BASA    11131225303   151-2006010  -4--313100010  1950   70000 1960062
171001  KAMUK   11131245030   001-2200015  4---311023211  1920   22000 1949062
171002  RESHE   112132245003  07--4017001  --4-311113020  1920   20000 1931062
063     JOS PLATEAU
170014  KATAB   111132245030  17--4215322  --4-314103250  1930   18000 1949063
170610  ANAGU   111131225133  35--2225325  -4--313113234  1920    5700 1934063
171006  KAGAR   111131245032  37--4246015  --4-311110020  1920   10000 1921063
171007  KAGOR   111131245033  17--4206012  --4-311113050  1920   10500 1950063
064     TIV-JUKUN
170115  JUKUN   111131225033  171-4645001  -2--841100033  1920   25000 1931064
170116  TIV     111132225233  051-2256342  -4--443113123  1920  700000 1952064
170215  MAMBI   11141245999   071-2235305  -2--443110100  1920   18000 1931064
065     WUTE
170353  WUTE    111132225231  161-4606205  --4-311100120  1910   30000     065
066     CHAMBA-YUNGUR
171017  LONGU   11231141030   371-2055005  -4--721100310  1920   12000 1921066
171018  MUMUY   11131241030   061-4246305  -4--311120010  1910   65000 1932066
171020  YUNGU   11231141030   051-2206005  -4--311100010  1920    9000 1921066
067     MANDARA HIGHLANDS
170315  MATAK   11141245939   052-2125012  --2-311100110  1940  100000 1958067
171023  GUDE    11141245030   05--4545015  --4-311100150  1920   30000 1958067
171025  KAPSI   11141245030   051-4246012  4---311100110  1930   25000 1950067
171026  PODOK   11141241230   351-4122212  4---311020110  1950   10000 1950067
```

```
COLS    COLS    COLS      COLS      COLS      COLS   COLS    COLS
1 - 6   7-11   12 - 23   24 - 34   35 - 47   61-64  65 - 73 74 - 80


068    ADAMAWA
181027 FALI   111131225030 15--2245015 4---311113210 1950     20000 1952068
181029 MBUM   121123225001 001-2046210 --4-311020330 1920     25000 1960068
181030 MUNDA  111231121003 061-4046015 4---311000230 1900     90000 1960068
069    LOGONE
180646 MASA   112132241031 352-2005312 --4-311100310 1910    125000 1957069
070    BAGIRMI-SARA
181036 BAGIR  111131221203 001-4604430 4---311000050 1880     26000 1954070
181037 SARA   11231121030 05--2201002 4---311000210 1890            070
071    BANDA-BAYA
180015 BANDA  111131225032 061-2245002 4---313100030 1920            071
180316 BAYA   111132225131 261-4245302 4---311110020 1910    200000 1930071
181038 BWAKA  111141225031 061-4246012 4---311110231 1920    180000 1940071
181041 NGBAN  111132225030 061-4241012 4---311000010 1920    115000 1958071
072    AZANDE
180117 AZAND  111132226232 961-2647221 4---411113224 1920    750000 1949072
073    MANGBETU
180702 MANGB  111132225233 061-2643001 4---411100320 1900    500000      073
181043 POPOI  111131225333 061-4216005 4---311100220 1910      5500 1912073
074    MORU-MADI
180217 MAMVU  111131225039 061-4201212 4---311020030 1920     33000 1949074
181044 LENDU  11231121233 351-4042014 2---311120120 1920    150000      074
181045 LESE   111131225033 061-4042012 4---311013131 1920     19000 1949074
181047 LUGBA  11231121000 351-2246012 -4-311100210 1920    240000 1948074
181048 MADI   111222121000 331-2046012 -4-311010210 1940     66000 1948074
181050 BONGO  111132225133 061-2112012 4---311120210 1870      5000 1929074
075    NUBA
180647 OTORO  111131241039 351-2456005 4---311110210 1940     40000 1947075
181053 KORON  11231121030 35--2005001 2---721100310 1930     14000 1947075
181054 MESAK  11231121030 35--2406001 2---721100310 1940      6000 1947075
181055 MORO   11231141030 35--2455005 -4-311100010 1940     20000 1947075
181056 TIRA   11231141030 35--2206005 4---311100010 1930      8000 1947075
181057 TULLI  11231121030 35--2246001 2---331100010             3500 1947075
076    FUNG
180218 SHILL  111132221030 001-2826315 4---311113210 1900    110000 1948076
181059 ANUAK  111132245030 05--4042302 4---311100210 1920     35000 1957076
077    KOMA
181061 KOMA   111132225033 05--4241002 2---313100010 1930      3000 1938077
181062 MAO    111132221030 00--4042012 4---313120130 1930      6000 1939077
078    NORTHERN NILOTES
181051 JUR    111131221031 361-2222302 4---311100320 1920            078
190120 NUER   111321121233 71--3155032 --4-411103210 1930    430000 1931078
190677 DINKA  11321121033 711-3206015 -4-311100210 1900    500000 1952078
079    BARI-LOTUKO
190354 BARI   111231121933 353-2341012 4---311110210 1920     35000 1952079
190678 LOTUK  111222121032 311-4346325 4---311110310 1920     60000 1940079
191065 KUKU   11231141033 351-2646012 4---311100210 1900     26000 1952079
191066 MONDA  111132221033 351-3345002 2---311000210 1930     22000 1962079
080    SOUTHERN NILOTES
190219 LANGO  11231121939 361-4445221 ---4311103310 1920    275000 1947080
190318 LUO    11131241931 351-2346212 --4-311112213 1940    800000 1947080
191067 ALUR   111132221030 351-2646012 --4-311120210 1890    200000      080
081    BEIR-DIDINGA
191068 BODI   111321121039 51--2042010 ---4011023210 1950      2600 1950081
191069 DIDIN  111221121039 321-3247001 4---311010020 1920     25000 1920081
191070 SURI   11231121039 301-4042011 4---311000000 1940      4000 1947081
082    KARAMOJONG
190017 TESO   11231121033 36--2206015 4---311100010 1950    560000 1948082
190220 TURKA  111222121233 12--3151024 --4-311103010 1920     80000 1951082
191071 JIE    111231121039 36--3306021 -4-311110210 1930     18000 1948082
191073 PSUK   111321121139 52--3156012 4---311110230 1950     42000 1948082
191074 TOPOT  111321121039 721-3046010 4---311010210 1930     34000 1948082
083    NANDI
190319 NANDI  111331141039 562-2112011 2---311102340 1910    113000 1948083
190648 KIPSI  11231141030 151-2157011 4---311110330 1920            083
191076 HSUK   11231141139 161-2122011 4---311100030 1910     20000 1948083
084    DOROBO
100101 DOROB  231114256279 99--1121142 1---311102040 1920       221 1942084
085    MASAI
190119 MASAI  111411251939 591-1156201 4---311112333 1900    187000 1948085
```

```
COLS      COLS      COLS       COLS        COLS       COLS     COLS     COLS
1 - 6     7-11      12 - 23    24 - 34     35 - 47    61-64    65 - 73  74 - 80

                            CIRCUM MEDITERRANEAN

086    SOUTHERN CUSHITES
200221 IRAQW  11331141999 771-2056200 2---331000050 1950      100000 1948086
087    AFAR-SOMALI
200019 SOMAL  11411242939 504-1427132 --4-311112325 1950     3000000     087
200649 AFAR   11411212000 501-3407232 --4-311320030 1880      110000 1950087
088    GALLA
200841 ARUSI  11321121039 531-3223010 4---311120050 1890             088
200842 GIBE   11231141039 372-2604030 2---311020020 1880             088
200843 MACHA  11231141039 372-2047015 2---311100040 1950             088
201090 JIMMA  11231141030 175-2858030 --4-311100050 1930      300000 1936088
089    SIDAMO
200707 GURAG  11231141030 072-4005012 --5-311000020 1940      350000 1960089
200844 BURJI  11131241039 173-2240014 4---311020040 1950             089
200845 DARAS  11131241039 152-2043001 4---314000040 1930             089
200846 SIDAM  11231141039 153-2002011 4---311020040 1930             089
090    KONSO
200018 KONSO  11231141039 353-4146001 ---4314100340 1930             090
200847 TSAMI  11231141039 35--2002000 4---311020030 1950        1000 1951090
091    NORTH RUDOLF
200849 BANNA  11321121039 711-2046012 -4--311020230 1950        5000 1950091
092    WESTERN CUSHITES
200853 BAKO   11231141039 353-2043010 4---311003010 1950             092
200858 BASKE  11231141099 371-2002010 2---311100010 1950        5000 1951092
200859 JANJE  11141241030 073-2644020 2---311000020 1920             092
200860 KAFA   11131241033 304-2608010 4---311120020 1890      500000 1905092
093    CENTRAL ETHIOPIA
200121 TIGRI  11231141039 371-4817431 1---312100020 1950     1000000     093
200679 AMHAR  11231141033 175-2818434 -1--444123123 1950     2000000     093
200861 FALAS  11231141000 371-4310030 1---444020120 1860       20000     093
094    BAREA-KUNAMA
200862 BAREA  11131221000 35--4251000 4---221110220 1860        9500 1937094
200863 KUNAM  11131221000 35--4251000 2---221110220 1860       17000 1937094
095    BEJA
200320 BISHA  11411242039 72--3156032 2---311300020 1930       15000 1933095
096    NUBIANS
180317 DILLI  11231141239 35--2206005 4---311200230 1930        8000     096
181058 NYIMA  11231141239 36--2205001 4---311100240 1930       37000 1947096
230024 BARAB  11231141093 171-4405231 2---311300025 1920             096
097    BAGGARA
210222 HASAN  11331121939 77--3400031 4---311300050 1920             097
098    DARFUR
210875 FUR    11231141032 152-4648034 -2--121110230 1880      120000 1937098
099    LAKE CHAD
210321 BUDUM  11221322109  001-2252000 4---311300030 1910       16000 1937099
100    BORNU
210876 KANEM  11231141030 072-4606031 -4--443300020 1930       30000 *937100
210877 KANUR  11131241000 151-4608431 4---441520150 1870             100
101    BOLEWA-TERA
210355 TERA   11131222931 051-4606005 -4--311200120 1920       38000 1948101
210680 BOLEW  11131221030 051-4607031 4---311200250 1920       33000 1933101
102    HAUSA
210682 KANAW  11131221909 171-4607435 --4-311300120 1940     1000000     102
211084 ZAZZA  11231141033 372-4848435 4---311313220 1950      260000 1948102
103    PASTORAL FULANI
210681 BOROR  11141221999 70--3411204 4---441110120 1920      450000     103
211079 DJAFU  11411211239 59--1200001 4---311200220 1930             103
211082 WODAA  11411211999 70--1046233 4---311313230 1950             103
104    SONGHAI
210122 SONGH  11231141933 077-4848431 2---311312020 1940      400000 1953104
105    TUAREG
220650 ANTES  11131242039 302-1626031 1---421310020 1910       10000 1941105
220880 AHAGG  11321142239 501-3637232 1---821210120 1920        4400 1950105
220881 ASBEN  11321142239 511-3637231 2---421200150 1900       28000 1944105
106    TEDA
220023 TEDA   11231142239 164-3616234 4---311120030 1950       25000     106
107    OASIS BERBERS
220123 SIWAN  11231141999 371-4456433 --2-311320025 1920        3000 1937107
220223 MZAB   11141245999 371-4655435 1---311020120 1920       32000 1939107
```

```
COLS   COLS      COLS         COLS          COLS        COLS    COLS     COLS
1 - 6  7-11      12 - 23      24 - 34       35 - 47     61-64   65 - 73  74 - 80


108    BEDOUIN ARABS
270022 REGEI  111311242033 732-3828032 --2-311300120 1950    35000 1950108
220887 CHAAM  111311242239 701-3643230 4---311300220 1930    20000 1936108
220888 DELIM  111312242033 733-1608031 --2-311300020 1930     6000 1915108
220891 ZENAG  111231142093 371-3627030 1---311300050 1910                108
290132 RWALA  11411252239  791-1406031 4---311320121 1920    35000 1920108
290414 MUTAI  11411252939  791-1006033 2---311320020 1930                108
109    MOROCCAN BERBERS
230125 RIFFI  111231141933 172-4356432 -2--311512120 1920   400000 1921109
230322 SHLUH  11231141230  372-2126035 --1-311020150 1920   600000 1921109
110    CANARY ISLANDS
230897 GUANC  111131225033 05--4537000 -1--421300000 1500                110
111    ALGERIAN BERBERS
230224 KABYL  11231141299  051-4228335 --2-311300150 1890  1000000 1930111
112    ARABS OF LITTORAL NORTH AFRICA
230124 EGYPT  111231141993 375-4828433 --2-311322124 1950 23000000 1957112
230898 ALGER  11231141000  171-4850435 --2-311320120 1870                112
113    ANCIENT EGYPT
230892 AEGYP  111131241030 373-4844440 1---241310104 BC   2000000        113
114    GREEKS
240708 GREEK  111231141993 35324724431 1---442100110 1950                114
115    ALBANIANS
240025 GHEG   111231141299 352-2147334 --4-311220110 1900   200000 1930115
116    ITALIANS
240611 NEAPO  111141241931 15124724433 1---244111114 1960                116
117    PEOPLES OF SPANISH AND PORTUGUESE SPEECH
240652 SPANI  111231141933 37224714431 1---244320114 1950                117
250356 BRAZI  111131241033 37114824431 1---244110110 1940                117
118    BASQUES
240225 BASQU  111231141993 371-2700031 ---1842000110 1930                118
119    FRENCH-SPEAKING PEOPLES
251133 FRCAN  111131241033 17134724431 1---242120114 1930                119
120    ENGLISH-SPEAKING PEOPLES
250027 NEWEN  111231141933 37434724431 1---244311114 1920                120
250226 TRIST  112122241333 13--4151233 1---244010110 1930      188 1938120
260128 IRISH  111231141930 371-2703431 ---1442120114 1930                120
121    PEOPLES OF DUTCH AND GERMAN SPEECH
260028 DUTCH  111231141993 37344728431 --1-844310114 1950                121
122    SCANDINAVIANS
260029 ICELA  112213210933 03--4600001 --1-442000110 1100                122
123    LAPPS
260129 LAPPS  111312253231 59--1301134 1---444112111 1950      191 1951123
124    FINNIC PEOPLES
270323 CHERE  111231141030 051-2506331 1---242100000 1900   400000 1941124
125    BALTO-SLAVS
271134 LITHU  111231141033 27214728431 --1-442100114 1930     2700 1950125
126    EASTERN SLAVS
270130 HUTSU  111221141930 131-2300433 1---242010115 1890    60000 1890126
270228 CZECH  11231141939  25234704431 ---144210114 1940  8800000 1950126
270685 BYELO  11231141033  17114708431 ---1842100114 1910                126
270686 UKRAI  11231141233  27114728433 ---1442100110 1930                126
127    HUNGARY-ROMANIA
271106 HUNGA  111131241900 071-4708433 -1--443120114 1940  9400000 1950127
128    SOUTH SLAVS
270030 SERBS  11231141939  253-4728435 --1-312020114 1950                128
270357 BULGA  11411241933  511-4708431 --1-444001110 1940  7000000 1950128
129    KIPCHAK TURKS
280131 KUMYK  11231141090  001-4000033 2---241000050 1900   135000 1959129
130    CIRCASSIANS
280229 CHERK  11231141939  371-2646031 --4-311000350 1920   250000        130
131    OSSET
280908 OSSET  11321141030  021-4646032 -2--311500010                     131
132    CHECHENO-LESGHIANS
280909 CHECH  11133141030  071-4000032 --4-311000050 1900   400000 1939132
133    GEORGIANS
280032 KHEVS  11231141033  361-4151002 2---311100000 1930     3500 1927133
134    ARMENIANS
280912 ARMEN  11231141030  171-4328431 -1--441100010 1900  3400000 1952134
```

```
COLS    COLS    COLS      COLS      COLS     COLS   COLS     COLS
1 - 6   7-11    12 - 23   24 - 34   35 - 47  61-64  65 - 73  74 - 80


135   KURD
280913 KURD  111231141933 373-3547033 2---311320120 1940  5000000 1950135
136   OTTOMAN TURKS
280653 TURKS 111231141033 371-4724433 ---2441220154 1950          136
137   JEWS
290230 HEBRE 111231141933 371-4607030 --4-311322020 BC           137
138   SEDENTARY ARABS OF THE NEAR EAST
290033 SYRIA 111231141939 37114527431 --2-311300124 1950          138
290417 LEBAN 111131241003 07214728433 1---314100000 1950  1575000 1956138
290914 DRUZE 11114l241139 372-4216335 --1-311322131 1930     600 1930138
139   MARSH ARABS
291091 MADAN 112123241303 233-4610435 --4-311300050 1950   400000     139
140   ANCIENT MESOPOTAMIA
290413 BABYL 111131241000 371-4804440 1---844020000 BC            140


                          EAST EURASIA


141   IRANIANS
301135 IRANI 111231141990 172-4618431 -2--411320154 1950 10000000    141
142   SOUTH IRAN NOMADS
300358 BASSE 111411215239 701-1342333 2---311320124 1950   16000 1957142
301107 BAKHT 11141l241039 732-1647032 ----311000050 1920          142
143   INDUS VALLEY
300034 SINDH 111231141030 373-4008433 --2-311320150 1950  9500000 1961143
144   HAZARA
300231 HAZAR 111331141999 771-3446231 --2-311320150 1930   65000     144
300709 MOGHO 111231141099 371-2020233 --2-311320120 1950    5500     144
145   PUSHTU
300133 PATHA 111231141999 372-4817331 2---311300020 1950  450000     145
146   DARD
300232 KOHIS 111221141139 113-3056035 2---311000120 1950   15000     146
300324 NURI  111231141039 363-4446301 --4-311100100 1890   60000     146
340327 DARD  111231141939 364-3607341 -4--311101114 1870            146
147   BURUSHO
340139 BURUS 111231141999 352-4006331 --2-314123153 1930   21000 1931147
148   TURKESTAN
310035 KAZAK 111411212939 711-3608232 --4-311110224 1910  2000000    148
149   MONGOLS
280031 KALMU 111311211239 731-3048002 -1--313100100 1920   70000 1939149
310036 MONGU 111231141933 152-2646005 --2-311210110 1920   55000 1909149
310134 KHALK 111411211939 531-3648101 ---1311100110 1940    2000     149
310687 CHAHA 111411211039 531-3607241 -1--311200110 1930    2300 1943149
150   SAMOYED
320136 YURAK 122213253233 39--1305124 --2-311522110 1900   13000     150
151   OSTYAK
321109 OBOST 122214253033 39--3405001 2---311100110 1880   17000 1897151
152   YENISEIANS
320360 KET   123114253037 39--3151200 1---411000010 1900    1300     152
153   YAKUT
320038 YAKUT 111213211233 322-3427222 --4-313510114 1900  245000 1911153
154   YUKAGHIR
320236 YUKAG 132114256073 99--3215104 ---2641101110 1900    1000 1900154
155   PALEO-SIBERIANS
320135 CHUKC 112313253233 791-1415121 ---4441311112 1900   12000 1900155
320235 KORYA 113214253237 391-3415221 -2--441122111 1900    7500 1900155
156   GILYAK
320037 GILYA 123114256237 991-3141215 2---311410110 1920    4650 1897156
157   AINU
320325 AINU  122114226231 92--3146143 --2-424512111 1900   17000     157
158   TUNGUS
321108 GOLDI 122114224931 02--4206000 --2-311200010 1920     100 1930158
159   MANCHURIA
330137 MANCH 111131241292 371-4420002 -1--311200010 1920            159
160   KOREA
330039 KOREA 111131241933 351-4817444 ---1314110114 1950   30000     160
161   JAPAN
330237 JAPAN 111131241993 35324728401 ---1444321114 1950   80000000  161
```

```
COLS    COLS     COLS          COLS          COLS      COLS    COLS       COLS
1 - 6   7-11     12 - 23       24 - 34       35 - 47   61-64   65 - 73    74 - 80


162     RYUKYU ISLANDS
330326  OKINA  11131241993 152-4527441 ---1314110112 1950     517000 1950162
163     NORTH CHINA
331110  SHANT  11131241990 351-4018405 --1-312500114 1930               163
164     SOUTH CHINA
330238  MINCH  11131241993 271-4818403 --2-311201112 1920               164
165     HAINAN
330710  LI     11131241033 15--4047244 ---2311010115 1930     220000 1954165
166     MIAO-YAO
330138  MIAO   11131241933 271-2116205 2---311210110 1940      10000 1940166
167     LOLO-NOSU
330040  LOLO   11231141939 151-4645242 2---311210110 1940               167
168     MINCHIA
330361  MINCH  11131241993 052-4326343 --2-311320110 1930     400000 1950168
169     UPPER BRAHMAPUTRA
340041  ABOR   11122221231 331-4455241 2---411410311 1940               169
170     TIBET
340239  TIBET  11231141933 153-4828441 ---3312500110 1920    4000000 191517u
171     SIKKIM
340140  LEPCH  11231141239 15--2446224 --2-311111111 1930               171
172     NEPAL
340630  SHERP  11331141909 752-3427341 3---312110110 1950               172
173     KASHMIR
351092  KASHM  11131241233 377-4008431 --2-311322121 1890    1700000 1941173
174     NORTH INDIA
350612  PAHAR  11231141093 273-4728441 --2-311120110 1950    5000000    174
351136  GUJAR  11131241992 154-4008446 2---311220110 1920    2200000 1921174
175     BHIL
350328  BHIL   11132241231 371-2746224 --2-311122111 1900    1250000    175
176     MUNDA
350042  SANTA  11131241233 352-4146014 --2-311120110 1940    2730000 1941176
360329  HILLB  11132221233 35--5042212 1---311210311 1930               176
360363  KOL    11131241299 371-4026004 --2-341100110 1940      94000 1941176
360654  BAIGA  11132226231 95--5101202 4---311211310 1930               176
177     NORTHERN DRAVIDIANS
350362  ORAON  11131241233 35--4026004 --2-311100310 1940     650000 1951177
360142  MARIA  11132225233 35--4346222 -4--311211310 1930      12000 1938177
361137  MURIA  11132221233 17--4100011 --2-311213311 1940     220000 1941177
178     INDIAN HUNTERS AND GATHERERS
360043  CHENC  411114211533 33--3125144 1---811211115 1940     3280 1941178
179     SOUTHEAST INDIA
360044  TAMIL  11131241990 375-4708401 --2-312200110 1880    3000000 1950179
360242  COORG  11131241933 071-2847246 --1-314222111 1930      40000 1936179
360688  TELUG  11231141933 176-4708441 --2-312210110 1950               179
180     NILGIRI HILLS
360143  TODA   11411251299 79--3126142 3---334212111 1900               180
181     SOUTHWEST INDIA
360243  KERAL  11231141933 372-2737401 -2--124200310 1800               181
182     SINHALESE
370245  SINHA  11231141000 071-4708401 1---442210110 1950               182
183     VEDDA
370145  VEDDA  222114256133 99--3105142 --1-524211115 1900              183
184     MALAGASY
370046  MERIN  11131241132 362-4618401 2---434210121 1900    1000000 1951184
370144  TANAL  11131241933 351-4626216 --4-334211123 1930     170000 1951184
370613  ANTAN  11222121032 311-3642013 4---311110133 1900     255000 1951184
370614  SAKAL  11321121933 711-2648312 -4--314110130 1900     275000 1951184
185     NICOBAR ISLANDS
370244  NICOB  11132234233 272-2125101 2---644110111 1890       9000 1924185
186     ANDAMAN ISLANDS
370045  ANDAM  212114256231 99--3121141 1---844110311 1870     5500 1858186
187     CHITTAGONG HILLS
380417  MOGH   11131221933 35--4006001 2---311200000 1880      66000 1951187
380418  CHAKM  11131221033 35--4002002 2---311100110 1870     125000 1951187
```

```
COLS    COLS    COLS      COLS      COLS    COLS   COLS      COLS
1 - 6   7-11    12 - 23   24 - 34   35 - 47 61-64  65 - 73   74 - 80


188     KUKI-CHIN
380147 LAKHE   111132221933 151-4646031 2---311210313 1930    10000      188
380247 PURUM   111131221939 151-4055241 ---2311422310 1930      300 1936188
380419 AIMOL   111132221033 051-4325211 2---311410310 1910      500 1931188
380711 CHIN    111132221033 051-4646041 2---311400110 1940   350000 1943188
189     GARO
380047 GARO    111141221131 15--4436211 ---2524210215 1900   160000 1901189
190     KHASI
380365 KHASI   111132221231 363-4626215 -1--524200111 1900   175000 1901190
191     NAGA
380048 LHOTA   111132221933 371-4445045 4---311400311 1920    20000 1922191
380421 ANGAM   111131241933 051-4445445 1---314010312 1910               191
380422 AO      111131221933 051-4451325 1---314410310 1920    30000 1921191
380424 SEMA    111132221933 051-4505315 2---311420310 1910               191
192     KACHIN
380246 KACKI   111131221239 271-4646225 --2-311410110 1940   300000      192
193     PALAUNG-WA
380426 PALAU   111141221999 351-4042243 2---441010010 1920   100000      193
391094 LAWA    111141221931 351-4016345 ---1311410110 1960     9000 1961193
194     BURMESE
380146 BURME   111131241933 375-4814443 1---642310110 1950 10000000 1931194
195     KAREN
380364 KAREN   111132241331 05--4445011 1---644100015 1910               195
196     THAI
390367 SIAME   111131241931 152-4828441 ---2644320114 1940 18000000 1957196
197     AKHA
390330 AKHA    111132221131 161-5141341 2---314110010 1950    65000      197
198     LAMET
390049 LAMET   111132221233 15--4345245 2---311410310 1940     5800      198
199     MUONG
391112 MUONG   111132241233 053-2547042 --2-311100110         250000 1946199
200     VEITNAMESE
390149 ANNAM   111131241003 074-4828445 --4-314123114 1950 22000000      200
201     MOI
390050 MNONG   111132221231 151-5455245 2---523400110 1940      146 1948201
202     CHAM-JARAI
390456 RHADE   111141221233 171-2335045 -2--522202110 1950   120000 1960202
390712 CHAM    111141241990 071-2027341 ---2524100010 1950   100000 1951202
203     KHMER
390248 CAMBO   111132241003 251-4824441 2---241320110 1950  3500000 1950203
204     SEMANG
390148 SEMAN   222114256133 99--1141124 2---444113111 1920               204
205     SENOI
391138 SENOI   111132226131 95--5155241 -2--844113115 1960    12000 1961205
206     MALAYS
390366 MALAY   111131241033 351-4607031 --2-441320150 1940  1250000      206
207     SEA GYPSIES
390249 SELUN   114114256937 99--1101001 2---244000110 1920               207
401099 TAWIT   114114235997 02--1341301 1---841300150 1960     1425 1963207


                         INSULAR PACIFIC

208     FORMOSAN ABORIGINES
400051 ATAYA   111132224333 261-4226241 ---1411120111 1930    33000 1931208
400331 PAIWA   111132224033 261-4546343 ---2441100311 1930    35000 1960208
401095 AMI     111131241033 351-4025345 --1-524100310 1930    55000 1960208
401096 BUNUN   121132224039 261-2045015 --1-311100010 1930    18000 1931208
401097 PUYUM   111131241033 361-4021303 1---644100310 1930     5300 1931208
401100 YAMI    112132225233 251-4151301 1---444100010 1930     1560 1960208
209     HIGHLAND LUZON
400052 SAGAD   111231141931 351-4355441 1---843112211 1950    10000      209
400150 IFUGA   111132244002 061-2455241 1---841410310 1920   130000 1939209
401139 KALIN   111132241133 151-2326311 --1-644110215 1910    24500 1939209
210     CENTRAL FILIPINOS
401098 SUGBU   111131241033 051-4724431 1---241102110 1950  2225000 1964210
```

```
COLS    COLS    COLS       COLS       COLS      COLS     COLS     COLS
1 - 6   7-11    12 - 23    24 - 34    35 - 47   61-64    65 - 73  74 - 80


211    SOUTHERN PHILIPPINES
400151 SUBAN  111141224333 05--2151141 2---841300110 1950      55000 1950211
400250 HANUN  111131221233 351-2151201 2---641100110 1950       6000 1950211
400368 TAGBA  111131221033 051-4651003 2---641100110 1950       7000    211
212    BORNEO
410053 IBAN   111131224133 351-4225041 ---1844310111 1950      11500 1947212
410251 DUSUN  111132221331 15--4325313 2---441110110 1920     145000    212
213    BATAK
410153 BATAK  111131241930 351-4445031 --2-311410200 1930    1000000 1959213
214    SUMATRAN MALAYS
410252 MINAN  111131241003 071-4637035 -2--124200250 1920    2000000 1930214
215    OFFSHORE SUMATRAN ISLANDS
410369 MENTA  111132234933 05--4155005 1---441510010 1930      10000 1930215
216    INDONESIAN HUNTERS AND GATHERERS
411114 KUBU   221114236030 90--1101000 2---841110110 1900       7000 1925216
217    JAVA
410054 JAVAN  111131241191 161-4724431 ---2644322130 1950   35000000 1956217
218    BALI
410152 BALIN  111231141093 371-4647003 --2-444300110 1950    1000000 1950218
219    SUMBA-SUMBAWA
421117 SUMBA  111131241030 061-4642002 ---2313400130 1930     100000 1940219
220    BUGINESE-MACASSARESE
420055 MACAS  111131241993 371-2648235 2---841312121 1940    4000000 1950220
221    CELEBES
420254 TORAD  111131221030 051-4426001 -1--641100110 1900     200000    221
222    FLORES
421115 ILIMA  112132225000 171-4607305 --2-311200111 1920             222
223    ALOR-SOLOR
420154 ALORE  111131224239 361-4407214 2---411112110 1940      10000 1940223
224    TIMOR-ROTI
420155 BELU   111231121030 351-2636005 -4--521400150 1950      82000 1952224
225    TANIMBAR
420332 TANIM  111132224333 261-4646001 --2-311200210 1930      25000    225
226    KEI-ARU
421116 KEI    111132234030 00--4245000 -2--311400010 1890      30000 1930226
227    MOLUCCAS
421140 AMBON  112132224000 051-4640435 1---411100150 1950      60000 1930227
228    HALMAHERA
421118 TOBEL  111132224031 05--4227004 -1--441100010 1910             228
229    NORTHWEST AUSTRALIA
430156 MURNG  321114256633 99--1141142 4---331421325 1930       1000 1950229
430157 TIWI   321114256631 99--1145211 --4-421120311 1920       1000    229
230    CENTRAL AUSTRALIA
430056 ARAND  321114256639 99--1141142 4---332121231 1900       2000 1900230
430255 DIERI  321114256633 99--1142144 4---423100221 1900             230
430256 KARIF  231114256273 99--1101102 4---333200210 1910        650 1865230
231    SOUTHEAST AUSTRALIA
431142 WONGA  222114256230 99--1141002 2---333100010 1910             231
232    TASMANIA
431141 TASMA  221114256232 99--1121144 2---0-4003015 1830             232
233    NORTHEAST AUSTRALIA
430333 WIKMU  221114256231 99--1101102 4---312400010 1920        150 1929233
234    SOUTHEAST NEW GUINEA
440631 MOTU   112133224033 15--4345345 --5-311113310 1950       7000 1954234
441143 KOITA  111132234033 05--4545041 2---311110310 1900       2000 1909234
441144 MAILU  112132234031 05--4105005 --1-313000310 1900             234
441145 MEKEO  111132234001 05--4545305 --4-311100310 1900       3100 1897234
441147 KOIAR  111132234030 05--4315005 4---311122010 1870             234
235    GULF OF PAPUA
440371 PURAR  211114234132 23--4346305 4---311100310 1910       8000    235
440656 KIWAI  111133236133 95--4155005 -2--313100110 1920             235
440657 MIRIA  112132234033 06--4151002 2---313100010 1900             235
236    MERAUKE
440247 KERAK  111131234931 25--3155242 4---313122311 1930        700 1926236
441101 KIMAM  111132244132 07--2105305 --2-413112312 1940       7000 1960236
441119 MARIN  111123234132 22--2155345 1---113122310 1910      13000 1910236
```

COLS	COLS	COLS	COLS	COLS	COLS	COLS	COLS
1 - 6	7-11	12 - 23	24 - 34	35 - 47	61-64	65 - 73	74 - 80

```
237    WEST PAPUANS
441153 MIMIK  212114236131 90--3105201 --1-523000010 1950       8500       237
238    WEST NEW GUINEA HIGHLANDS
440057 KAPAU  111131224932 25--4316212 --4-311111310 1950      60000 1955238
441146 MUJU   111132234033 25--2115142 --2-311100010 1950                 238
239    EAST NEW GUINEA HIGHLANDS
440334 ENGA   111131224939 26--2155302 2---311120210 1950      26000       239
440632 KAKOL  11131244139 26--2125312 ---2313113215 1950                   239
440691 KUTUB  211123234331 22--4105001 -4--111120310 1940        400 1940239
440713 SIANE  111131234139 26--5315342 0---111113300 1940      15000 1953239
240    EAST PAPUANS
440058 WANTO  111131234939 25--4115242 4---313203311 1920       5150 1954240
440457 OROKA  111133234133 16--4125245 2---311210110 1920       9000       240
441148 MAFUL  111131234033 25--2345045 4---311110311 1920       9000       240
441149 NGARA  111132234030 07--4125205 2---313103310 1940        600 1945240
241    NORTH PAPUANS
440158 ARAPE  111132234339 27--2151045 4---314122110 1930                 241
440655 KWOMA  211123234132 21--2155042 4---311113111 1930                 241
440690 ABELA  111132234030 25--4155045 2---311102010 1930                 241
441150 BANAR  111132234333 06--2155005 1---313200010 1910                 241
242    NORTHWEST NEW GUINEA MELANESIANS
440258 WAROP  212114234333 32--4215005 -2--313400000 1930       6000 1937242
243    NORTHEAST NEW GUINEA MELANESIANS
440159 WOGEO  111132234293 05--4145246 4---333113330 1930       1000       243
441151 BUSAM  111132234033 06--4315045 2---433120310 1940       1300 1946243
441152 MANAM  112132234033 06--2145045 2---314100310 1930       3500 1933243
244    PALAU
450059 PALNS  112132234993 06--4537045 2---721110112 1940       6000 1960244
245    YAP
450260 YAPES  112132234993 261-2736005 --1-334113310 1910       3700 1935245
246    MARIANAS ISLANDS
450427 CHAMO  111131221993 052-4122331 1---244121110 1950                 246
247    CENTRAL CAROLINE ISLANDS
450060 TRUKE  113133234995 27--2135245 -1--524113312 1940      10000 1947247
450161 IFALU  112132234293 251-4136245 -1--824112113 1940        250 1948247
450428 ULITH  112132234003 06--4136203 1---421100310 1900        420 1949247
450692 CAROL  113133234997 06--2105005 -1--524112310 1930       1100 1950247
248    EASTERN CAROLINE ISLANDS
450259 PONAP  112132234993 071-2537141 2---524212010 1910       8000 1935248
450430 KUSAI  112132234991 07--2507011 2---424210210 1860        500 1905248
249    NAURU
450432 NAURU  112132236931 95--2506301 --2-524200010 1900       3300       249
250    MARSHALL ISLANDS
450160 MAJUR  112132234993 07--4536045 -1--824211111 1940        900 1947250
450431 BIKIN  112132234991 07--4156205 --1-524200010 1940        170 1935250
251    GILBERT ISLANDS
450372 ONOTO  113123234197 91--4426305 2---441120100 1940                 251
450633 MAKIN  112123234933 12--4516315 2---443121221 1890       2000 1890251
252    WESTERN ISLANDS OF BISMARCK ARCHIPELAGO
461154 AUA    113123236037 93--4246005 4---124310300 1900                 252
253    ADMIRALTY ISLANDS
460373 MANUS  11414214297 29--4355245 2---333120311 1920       2000 1929253
460615 USIAI  111131234339 26--4105245 4---333100311 1950                 253
254    NEW IRELAND
460163 LESU   112123234933 22--2115345 2---521103321 1930                 254
255    NEW BRITAIN
460335 LAKAL  111123234331 21--2325205 --4-821200310 1950                 255
256    MASSIM
460062 TROBR  112132234233 25--4532245 2---723213311 1910                 256
460261 DOBUA  112132234933 05--4155002 1---823113200 1920                 256
461155 DAHUN  112132234031 05--2335341 -2--823102350 1900        250 1951256
257    LOUISADE ARCHIPELAGO
460693 ROSSE  212124234333 02--4345111 2---421103010 1920       1500 1925257
258    BUKA
460162 KURTA  111132234233 26--2535244 4---821113311 1930                 258
```

COLS 1 - 6	COLS 7-11	COLS 12 - 23	COLS 24 - 34	COLS 35 - 47	COLS 61-64	COLS 65 - 73	COLS 74 - 80

```
259   BOUGAINVILLE
460061 SIUAI  111132234231 25--2315045 2---721213110 1940    4650 1938259
260   CHOISEUL-EDDYSTONE
461102 CHOIS  111132234030 05--2445045 2---441110300 1900    1000 1956260
261   MALAITA-ULAWA
460262 ULAWA  112132234933 251-2145245 2---441120312 1900    1200 1909261
262   SANTA CRUZ ISLANDS
471156 SANTA  112132234033 162-4415001 --2-421220300 1930    2500 1958262
263   BANKS ISLANDS
470063 MOTA   112132234993 30--4315045 4---721100311 1890         263
264   MALEKULA
470064 SENIA  112132234933 35--4341002 4---311100311 1930         264
265   AMBRYM-PENTECOST
470164 BUNLA  111131234000 30--4355245 2---333123321 1950      90 1953265
266   SOUTHERN NEW HEBRIDES
471157 TANNE  111131234030 05--4542002 2---311200350 1920         266
267   LOYALTY ISLANDS
470374 LIFU   112132234393 06--4646002 -4--311100300 1910         267
268   NEW CALEDONIA
470263 AJIE   112132244000 06--4146002 ----313200000 1860    1700 1955268
269   FIJI
470165 LAU    112132234231 37--4347242 --4-313213331 1920         269
470694 VANUA  112132234232 17--4106245 --2-333110030              269
270   ROTUMA
470337 ROTUM  111131234991 07--4546005 1---524110100 1890         270
271   POLYNESIAN OUTLIERS IN MICRONESIA
481103 KAPIN  112132234933 06--4546041 --2-844112310 1910     482 1950271
272   POLYNESIAN OUTLIERS IN CENTRAL MELANESIA
480265 ONTON  13133236997 961-3345041 -2--644100100 1920     700 1928272
273   POLYNESIAN OUTLIERS IN EASTERN MELANESIA
480066 TIKOP  13133236995 961-2546341 4---313110131 1930    1300 1929273
274   WESTERN POLYNESIANS
480065 SAMOA  112132234991 151-4547215 -2--843113122 1920    8000 1926274
480166 PUKAP  112132234391 16--4146215 1---333111111 1930     500  274
480264 ELLIC  13132234995 031-4506005 --2-443112301 1890          274
480375 TOKEL  13123236995 93--4146005 -2--443113330 1900     380 1930274
481120 FUTUN  112132234002 271-4526040 --2-444110331 1840    1500 1923274
481121 NIUEA  13133236095 95--4506345 2---444110031 1840    3720 1921274
481124 TONGA  112132234003 37--4547045 2---444112132 1850   24000 1921274
481125 UVEAN  112132234091 272-4547040 2---444110332 1830    4400 1919274
275   SOUTHERN POLYNESIANS
490167 MAORI  111123226333 931-4646015 --4-443110011 1820   90000 1940275
276   EASTERN POLYNESIANS
490067 MNGNS  112132236993 96--2546044 --4-444110141 1820    1250 1926276
490168 MARQU  112132234993 272-2546241 3---443211141 1900   15000 1840276
490266 MANIH  13133236995 90--4546040 --2-444310011 1850     400 1926276
490267 RAROI  113123236197 93--2146001 -2--844010000 1900     109 1950276
490376 HAWAI  112133244093 071-4646045 -2--844110004 1800          276
490658 MANGA  13123236097 912-4547041 2---444112031 1900          276
490659 TAHIT  112132234093 071-4547041 2---844110000 1900          276
491126 EASTE  111132226003 97--4642040 --2-444110000 1860     450 1936276
```

NORTH AMERICA

```
277   WESTERN ESKIMO
500269 NUNIV  123114256237 99--3355041 --2-444300211 1930          277
500458 ALEUT  123114256237 99--4645211 -4--441312112 1930    1500 1834277
500459 CHUGA  114114256237 99--4645041 ----444212212 1930     200 1933277
500460 SIVOK  114114253237 39--4005205 ---1311500111 1920     293 1955277
278   INTERIOR ESKIMO
500461 NUNAM  131114256273 29--3311241 ---2841111112 1950     200 1953278
500484 CAESK  132114256273 99--3111141 ---4841112112 1900     500 1923278
279   CENTRAL AND EASTERN ESKIMO
500069 TAREU  123114256935 99--3355241 --4-844110112 1880    1000 1880279
500169 CESKI  123114256237 99--3151143 1---241111112 1920          279
```

COLS 1 - 6	COLS 7-11	COLS 12 - 23	COLS 24 - 34	COLS 35 - 47	COLS 61-64	COLS 65 - 73	COLS 74 - 80

```
500462 BAFFI 114114256037 99--3121121 ---4241002112 1880          279
500463 PESKI 123114256137 99--3151141 2---844013211 1880      271 1926279
500485 IGLUL 133114256977 99--3115144 --2-444112112 1920      500 1922279
500486 LABRA 123114256237 99--3145101 --2-441010112 1890     1100 1890279
500487 ANGMA 114114256237 99--3155141 -2-444113111 1880       371 1884279
   280   CREE-MONTAGNAIS
500268 NASKA 131114256270 99--3111111 --2-844210110 1890          280
500338 ATTAW 123114256237 99--3125241 2---441200112 1900          280
500494 ECREE 132114256271 99--3121041 --2-644310112 1850          280
500495 MONTA 131114256271 99--3145241 -2--441222112 1880      670 1929280
   281   MARITIME ALGONKIANS
500504 MICMA 132114256073 99--3142111 1---411122112 1700     3000 1609281
   282   OJIBWA
500496 NSAUL 122114256233 99--3155241 --2-414203112 1870      900 1930282
500497 PEKAN 122114256033 99--3106102 ---2314210110 1940      342 1949282
500498 NIPIG 132114256273 99--3145210 --2-414200112 1800      820 1860282
500499 CHIPP 112114226232 92--3145241 --2-214220112 1860          282
500500 RAINY 22114256231 99--3155241 --2-811210112 1880      244 1917282
500501 KATIK 22114256233 99--3145214 --2-414221112 1800       76 1940282
500502 EOJIB 222114256233 99--3141242 2---411220112 1870      150 1929282
   283   NORTHEASTERN ATHAPASKANS
500464 DOGRI 123114256237 99--3121001 2---444000110 1860      900 1959283
500465 SATUD 123114256037 99--1121011 2---444010012 1860          283
500466 SLAVE 132114256273 99--3121211 4---441113112 1860      400 1881283
500491 SEKAN 132114256073 99--3121030 4---441100012 1880      160 1923283
500492 BEAVE 231114256270 99--3101143 2---644020010 1850      380 1914283
500493 CHIPE 132114256073 99--3151040 2---444101112 1880          283
   284   CARRIER-NAHANI
500170 KASKA 123114256235 99--3151245 -1--521412012 1920      300      284
500468 CARRI 122114256233 99--3655321 --4-521202112 1880      300 1925284
500490 TAHLT 132114256073 99--3435014 2---721013212 1870       50 1885284
   285   UPPER YUKON
500469 KUTCH 123114256037 99--3442141 4---424112112 1880      337 1958285
   286   LOWER YUKON
500377 INGAL 123114256237 99--3351011 2---644110011 1880          286
   287   SOUTH CENTRAL ALASKA
500068 NABES 131114256373 99--3121141 1---624220012 1930      152 1930287
500489 TANAI 123114256237 99--4545041 --4-421120312 1870      650 1932287
510270 EYAK  123114256237 99--4436141 4---721200312 1890       38 1933287
   288   TLINGIT-HAIDA
510070 HAIDA 113114256237 99--4635042 -2--721213312 1890     1000 1890288
510505 TLING 123114256237 99--3635342 --2-723611312 1880     6750 1880288
   289   TSIMSHIAN-HAISLA
510378 TSIMS 113114256237 99--3636041 -4--721200312 1880          289
510470 HAISL 123114256037 99--3635341 ---723220312 1880      400 1930289
   290   KWAKIUTL-BELLACOOLA
510171 KWAKI 213114256237 99--4646004 --2-443122112 1890          290
510471 COOLA 113114256237 99--4655211 --4-443111112 1880      300 1922290
510472 ALKAT 123114256237 99--3645041 --4-441110112 1865      100 1936290
510506 BELLA 123114256037 99--3635241 -2--443200112 1880      330 1901290
   291   NOOTKA-QUILEUTE
510473 NOOTK 113114256237 99--3646044 --2-443120112 1880     6000      291
510480 QUILE 123114256237 99--4645144 -4--441102012 1880      285 1945291
510507 MAKAH 113114256237 99--3645244 --2-443100112 1860      654 1861291
   292   COAST SALISH
510071 TWANA 123114256237 991-3415244 -2--443122112 1850      600 1850292
510475 SQUAM 123114256037 99--3455044 --4-441120112 1880          292
510477 LUMMI 213114256237 99--3605244 -4--443120112 1880          292
510478 KLALL 123114256237 99--3645244 --4-443120012 1860      485 1881292
510479 PUYAL 213114256237 991-3415141 --4-443110012 1870          292
510508 QUINA 123114256237 991-3615244 --2-444111112 1860      200 1925292
510509 COWIC 123114256237 99--3455044 --4-441120112 1880          292
510510 STALO 222114256233 99--3625144 --4-443120112 1880     1700 1951292
   293   CHINOOK
510481 CHINO 113114256237 99--4645000 --4-441103112 1850      100 1853293
530560 WISHR 213114256237 99--3445241 --4-443100112 1860     1000 1800293
```

```
COLS    COLS      COLS        COLS         COLS       COLS    COLS     COLS
1 - 6   7-11     12 - 23     24 - 34      35 - 47     61-64   65 - 73  74 - 80


294   OREGON SEABOARD
510271 TOLOW 212114256233 99--3441042 4---311222112 1870              294
510483 COOS  123114256030 99--4415004 -4--441100112 1860              294
510511 ALSEA 113114256237 99--4415004 --2-441100212 1860              294
510514 TUTUT 213114256037 99--3411002 4---311410012 1870              294
295   NORTHWEST CALIFORNIA
510172 YUROK 213114256237 99--4415144 --4-441102112 1850    2500 1850295
510515 SHAST 222114256233 99--3446144 --2-441100112 1860    2000 1850295
510516 CHIMA 222114256133 99--4345141 --2-841110012 1860     250 1849295
510517 KAROK 213114256237 99--4455044 --2-441112012 1860     600 1905295
510518 HUPA  213114256137 99--4445244 --4-441113012 1860     640 1870295
510519 WIYOT 213114256237 99--4455114 --4-441120012 1860     800 1853295
510522 SINKY 222114256233 99--4345221 --2-841112112 1860              295
296   NORTHEAST CALIFORNIA
520272 ATSUG 222114256233 99--3341244 --4-443121112 1860              296
520525 ACHOM 222114256233 99--3345001 --4-441112112 1860    1000 1900296
520526 YANA  312114256633 99--3345001 --2-441120112 1860      35 1884296
297   MAIDU-WINTUN
520072 NOMLA 321114256633 99--4341212 2---313110012 1850     300 1954297
520527 MAIDU 321114256633 99--3326111 --4-441100112 1850     250 1905297
520528 NISEN 321114256633 99--3341041 2---444121112 1850              297
520529 WINTU 222114256233 99--3341214 2---444102212 1860              297
520537 PATWI 321114256030 99--3345001 --2-811400212 1850     150 1924297
298   POMO-YUKI
520375 YUKI  222114256233 99--3341211 2---443112112 1850    2000   298
520530 CYUKI 212114256233 99--3121014 4---844111112 1860     500 1850298
520532 NPOMO 321114256533 99--3045041 --4-844111012 1860              298
520533 EPOMO 222114256233 99--3325211 --2-844100112 1860              298
520534 SPOMO 222114256030 99--3335001 --1-644100012 1860              298
520535 WAPPO 321114256633 99--3025201 --1-844110112 1860              298
299   MIWOK-YOKUTS
520174 YOKUT 222114256133 99--3345045 -4--314102112 1850     550 1910299
520273 MIWOK 321114256030 99--3141002 4---314102112 1850              299
520538 MONAC 321114256630 99--3341201 2---314102012 1870     500 1920299
520539 LAKEY 312114256630 99--3305042 -2--314100112 1860              299
520540 WUKCH 222114256233 99--3345001 --2-314102212 1860              299
300   KERN RIVER
520173 TUBAT 321114256633 99--3142141 1---441112010 1850     145 1932300
520542 KAWAI 321114256030 99--3311001 1---441000012 1860              300
301   SOUTHWEST CALIFORNIA
520544 GABRI 212114256230 99--3341012 2---314100012 1770    5000 1770301
520545 SERRA 321114256030 99--3145012 --4-311100012 1870     100 1910301
520546 CAHUI 321114256033 99--3145012 --2-314100012 1870     750 1920301
520547 CUPEN 321114256630 99--3141002 2---314100012 1870     200 1910301
520548 LUISE 311114256630 99--3141242 --4-311103112 1860    1300 1870301
302   DIEGUENO
520339 DIEGU 321114256639 99--3145242 --4-311102112 1850     700   302
520549 KILIW 222114256230 99--3141042 2---311100112 1880      36 1929302
303   WASHO
530340 WASHO 222114256231 99--3141141 2---844102112 1850     850 1960303
304   CENTRAL GREAT BASIN
530274 HUKUN 321114256530 99--3141043 --4-844100112 1870              304
530564 WADAD 321114256633 99--3121141 2---644112112 1870     200 1870304
530566 KIDUT 221114256233 99--3121101 4---841122112 1870     150 1873304
530569 KUYUI 312114256633 99--3121141 2---644102112 1860     700 1866304
530572 EMONO 321114256633 99--3145014 --2-444113112           1000 1870304
530574 PANAM 321114256633 99--3141101 2---644101112 1850      65 1870304
530585 WHITE 321114256633 99--3151111 --4-644210112 1860     800   304
530588 AGAID 222114256233 99--3121201 2---441112112 1860     600 1860304
530590 GOSIU 321114256633 99--3151101 2---644213112 1860              304
305   SOUTHERN PAIUTE
530591 ANTAR 321114256630 99--3121100 2---644113112 1860              305
530594 SHIVW 321114246639 93--3111001 2---844102112 1860     300 1873305
530595 KAIBA 321114246639 91--3121101 2---444112112 1860     600 1850305
530596 CHEME 321114246639 90--3141041 1---844102112 1860     350 1920305
530598 SANJU 321114242534 40--3121000 2---644112112 1860              305
```

COLS 1 - 6	COLS 7-11	COLS 12 - 23	COLS 24 - 34	COLS 35 - 47	COLS 61-64	COLS 65 - 73	COLS 74 - 80

```
306   PLATEAU YUMANS                                                        306
530175 HAVAS 211133246239 97--3145243 -2--444100112 1880             1000 1870306
530607 WALAP 321114212639 93--3145141 --2-444212112 1870              500 1870306
530608 YAVAP 321114216639 91--3111041 2---844102112 1870              500 1870306
530609 TOLKE 321114226039 91--3121241 4---841110112 1870                  306
570628 KEWEY 321114216633 22--3151001 2---824110110 1870
307   EASTERN GREAT BASIN                                                  307
530074 SUTE  231114212273 31--3141011 2---644113112 1860             1500 1867307
530587 BOHOG 231114252273 39--3321201 2---841110112 1860                  307
530600 UINTA 222114252233 09--3141001 2---644103012 1860                  307
530604 UNCOM 231114252273 39--1101201 2---644003112 1860             600 1869307
530605 BANNO 231114252273 09--3122204 2---644112112 1860            1600 1869307
530606 WINDR 231114252273 39--3122201 --2-641112112 1860
308   LUTUAMI
520523 KLAMA 213114256237 99--3425141 --2-443122112 1860            1200 1854308
520524 MODOC 321114256633 99--3425141 --2-443112112 1860             300 1910308
309   SAHAPTIN
530073 TENIN 213114256237 99--3441334 ---4443120112 1850            1200 1850309
530561 UMATI 222114252233 09--3222004 2---443122012 1860                  309
530562 NEZPE 222114252233 39--3426244 -2--441111212 1850            6000 1800309
310   INTERIOR SALISH
530176 SANPO 213114256237 99--3141221 ---4444111112 1870             660 1860310
530554 FLATH 222114252233 39--3242041 4---444113112 1860                  310
530556 COEUR 222114252233 09--3426241 --4-444122212 1860             500 1905310
530557 SINKA 222114252230 99--3141213 4---843110112 1880             300 1930310
311   NORTHERN PLATEAU
530550 CHILC 123114256237 99--3445101 --2-443111112 1880             600 1840311
530551 LILLO 123114256037 99--3445044 --4-444122112 1860            4000 1850311
530552 THOMP 123114256037 99--3445044 --4-443122212 1860                  311
530553 SHUSW 222114256233 99--3246241 --4-443122212 1850                  311
312   KUTENAI
530380 KUTEN 222114252233 39--3212011 2---444112112 1880            1200 1891312
313   NORTHWEST PLAINS
540075 GROSV 141114252279 39--1112034 4---441122012 1870                  313
540381 SARSI 141114252273 39--1112001 4---441122110 1880                  313
540619 BLACK 141114252279 39--1325314 --4-441121112 1850            1600 1809313
540620 BLOOD 141114252279 39--1322214 4---443111112 1850             800 1809313
540625 PIEGA 141114252279 39--1322314 4---443110112 1850            2800 1809313
314   NORTHEAST PLAINS
540382 TETON 141114252273 39--3216014 --4-441110012 1870                  314
540618 ASSIN 131114252273 39--1121314 4---441113012 1870            3000 1890314
540621 BUNGI 131114252273 39--1141311 2---014110112 1850            7000 1958314
540626 PLAIN 131114252273 39--1141011 2---441213112 1850                  314
540627 SANTE 131114212073 02--3101000 4---441100012 1850                  314
315   UPPER MISSOURI
540178 CROW  141114212279 30--3112044 4---424101012 1870            1800 1935315
540341 MANDA 121133242933 36--3106001 --4-524400110 1830                  315
540622 HIDAT 111132242230 36--3125311 --4-524100112 1860             471 1905315
316   SOUTHERN PLAINS
540076 KAPAC 141114252279 39--1105001 -4--643110110 1870             200 1934316
540177 COMAN 141114252279 39--1225003 -4--844100010 1870                  316
540275 CHEYE 141114212279 32--1156044 --4-644123112 1860            4700 1870316
540616 ARAPA 141114252279 39--3116344 -4--644123112 1860            2300 1904316
540624 KIOWA 141114252079 09--3116201 4---444100110 1860            1165 1905316
317   CADDO
550277 WICHI 121133222239 36--3146011 --4-641103110 1860             500 1950317
550384 HASIN 121133226230 96--2647031 -2--644100112 1770                  317
318   PAWNEE-ARIKARA
540617 ARIKA 121133242033 06--4047300 ---4-644000012 1860           1650 1871318
550342 PAWNE 121133222030 36--3646313 -4--524101312 1860           10000 1780318
319   PRAIRIE SIOUANS
550078 WINNE 121124226233 92--3146005 --2-311200210 1850                  319
550179 OMAHA 121123222231 32--3216245 2---313111112 1850            1200 319
550695 IOWA  131133222070 30--3546000 2---314000112 1870                  319
550696 OTO   131123222073 32--3505000 2---311100112 1870                  319
551104 PONCA 121124222233 32--3546000 2---314110112 1850             825 1880319
```

```
COLS    COLS    COLS      COLS        COLS      COLS    COLS     COLS
1 - 6   7-11    12 - 23   24 - 34     35 - 47   61-64   65 - 73  74 - 80


320   CENTRAL ALGONKIANS
500660 PCTAW  131124226070 92--3006010 4---314102112 1760         2000 1760320
550276 MIAMI  121123226230 92--3246320 4---313100012 1720         6000 1718320
550383 FOX    121123222030 32--3246031 -4--811100110 1830              320
550661 MENOM  211114226233 92--3206002 --4-314100012 1870         1600 1900320
551158 SHAWN  121124226030 92--3246031 --2-314110112 1820         1160 1930320
321   IROQUOIS
560079 HURON  112133226233 96--3336315 -1--524113112 1640        24000 1640321
560663 IROQU  121123226233 92--4137315 -1--524013212 1750              321
322   MIDDLE ATLANTIC ALGONKIANS
560279 DELAW  111123226233 92--3135325 -2--524010110 1700         8000 1600322
323   CHEROKEE-YUCHI
560278 CHERO  111133226233 96--4107305 --2-524100112 1750        20000 1729323
560664 YUCHI  111132226031 95--4126001 2---224000012 1750         1140 1832323
324   MUSKOGEE
560180 CREEK  111123226233 92--4137315 -2--524122012 1750        20000      324
560386 TIMUC  111123226030 92--3036045 -2--520000010 1560              324
561159 CHOCT  111123226030 92--2102001 2---524100110 1760        15000      324
325   LOWER MISSISSIPPI
560385 NATCH  121133226033 96--4036311 --4-444110011 1700         3000 1700325
326   TEXAS COAST
540623 KARAN  222114252233 99--1142000 2---841003011 1800          200 1814326
327   APACHE
570081 CHIRI  321114212639 31--1125041 --4-644123112 1880         1000 1880327
570439 MESCA  221114216230 92--3205001 --4-644100112 1870              327
570440 JICAR  221114222230 01--3145041 --4-644113112 1870              327
570697 LIPAN  321114252639 09--3126001 -1--644100112 1880              327
328   EASTERN PUEBLOS
570281 TAOS   111131242039 37--4121303 1---244110112 1890          700 1930328
570433 PICUR  111131240039 07--4121243 1---244100012 1920          100      328
570434 ISLET  111131245039 00--4121443 1---244100112 1920         1036 1930328
570435 TEWA   111141242030 07--4121343 1---244110010 1900          126 1937328
329   CENTRAL PUEBLOS
570343 COCHI  111132242033 07--4125343 --1-524101110 1890          600      329
570387 JEMEZ  111132242139 07--4125303 1---224100112 1920          650 1937329
570436 SANTA  111131241039 07--4325343 --1-824112110 1920          242 1934329
570716 SIA    111131241039 07--4125313 1---224102110 1920          327 1957329
330   WESTERN PUEBLOS
570082 HANO   111231141039 37--4105305 --1-524110110 1950          400 1950330
570183 ZUNI   111141245939 07--4125445 -1--524100110 1910         2250 1941330
570437 ACOMA  111131245039 07--4105403 -1--824100110 1920         1250 1941330
570442 HOPI   111131245239 37--4135341 -1--524112210 1920         3500 1950330
331   NAVAHO
570182 NAVAH  111222145239 131-3225341 --4-524112112 1930        50000 1950331
570441 WAPAC  221124222239 32--3135105 --2-524110112 1870         4700 1940331
332   RIVER YUMANS
570280 MARIC  211124246233 93--4106241 2---314100112 1850          700 1850332
570443 COCOP  111123242230 91--2225041 2---311112112 1850              332
570444 KAMIA  111123246030 91--2026041 2---314100012 1860          250 1849332
570445 MOHAV  211123246030 91--2246041 2---814110012 1850              332
570446 YUMA   111133246030 95--4021102 1---314101112 1860              332
333   PIMA-PAPAGO
580184 PAPAG  211133246239 97--3155031 --4-444101112 1930         5000      333
581160 PIMA   211133246130 97--4145001 --2-444100112 1840        20000      333
334   SERI
580283 SERI   113114256030 99--3105001 --1-441100110 1900          200 1960334
335   CAHITA
581161 YAQUI  111132246033 97--4125001 --2-444100112 1870              335
336   TARAHUMARA
580083 TARAH  111231141239 17--2321033 2---241111114 1930              336
337   HUICHOL
580282 HUICH  111132221333 17--2325303 --2-844300115 1920         4000      337
338   CHICHIMEC
580717 CHICH  321114256630 99--1121041 1---644122112 1570              338
339   TARASCANS
591163 TARAS  111132246030 97--4047005 --2-444300010 1550              339
340   TOTONAC
590285 TOTON  111132222233 17--4006400 ----444100110 1940       100000      340
```

```
COLS    COLS     COLS       COLS         COLS        COLS    COLS     COLS
1 - 6   7-11    12 - 23    24 - 34      35 - 47     61-64   65 - 73  74 - 80


341    AZTEC
590185 AZTEC  111132246933 975-4847425 2---444110014 1520                    341
342    PUEBLA NAHUATL
591164 TLAXC  11114221999 172-4110432 --2-414112115 1960    300000 1960342
343    CHINATEC-MAZATEC
590084 CHINA  111141225239  27--4025333 ---1444100110 1940    40000    343
344    MIXE-ZOQUE
590284 POPOL  111141224933  07--4121030 4---444100011 1940    10000    344
591162 MIXE   111141221933  37--4026035 --1-444012110 1930              344
345    MIXTEC-ZAPOTEC
591165 ZAPOT  111141220033 171-4020433 1---444100110 1940   215000 1950345


                        SOUTH AMERICA

346    LOWLAND MAYA
600186 CHORT  111131224233  17--4726014 --1-841100115 1930              346
600345 YMAYA  111132226933  97--4806401 1---411200312 1520              346
600665 LACAN  111132220033  07--2100012 --4-314020110 1900   200000 1900346
347    HIGHLAND MAYA
600389 MAM    111141222000  37--4310435 --1-314120110 1930              347
601166 QUICH  111141225033 171-4426035 2---314120110 1930    25000    347
348    LENCA-JICAQUE
601129 LENCA  111132224033  07--4541033 4---244000110                  348
349    MISKITO-ULVA
600390 MISKI  211114221133  02--4106231 -2--644221111 1920     6000 1944349
350    TALAMANCA
600287 BRIBR  111132224233  05--2101021 1---221212115 1950     4000 1960350
351    CUNA
600085 CUNA   112132224333 371-4426233 -2--641120115 1940    21000 1940351
352    CHOCO
600286 CHOCO  111132226033  95--2101213 1---244100110 1960     5000    352
353    ANTILLEAN ARAWAK
611130 TAINO  111132246033  96--4633010 --2-4-1010011 1520              353
354    ANTILLEAN CARIB
600388 BLCAR  112132236031  96--4111431 2---244202110 1940    30000    354
610087 CALLI  113123246237  92--2225015 -2--521212310 1650              354
355    SIERRA NEVADA DE SANTA MARTA
610187 CAGAB  111141224231  05--3345011 2---641100015 1940     2000 1941355
356    GOAJIRO
610391 GOAJI  111311211233  52--1435121 --4-721512011 1940    18000    356
357    PARAUJANO
610289 PARAU  213114256000  99--4101013 2---841110110 1950     1350 1958357
358    MOTILON
610718 YUPA   211133226133  95--4111111 2---644200110 1950      156 1954358
359    GUAHIBO
620290 GUAHI  121123226233  93--3125241 --2-641212111 1960    12000 1966359
360    MIDDLE ORINOCO
620089 YARUR  111123224233  33--4141003 ---2641201015 1950              360
361    SALIVA
620447 PIARO  122114226233  92--3101044 2---644200010 1950              361
362    SOUTH VENEZUELAN ARAWAK
620291 WAPIS  111123226233  92--4105004 4---441200111 1900              362
620448 CURIP  112133226233  96--4101103 1---440100010 1950              362
620719 PIAPO  111132226033  96--4105104 --4-444210010 1950      200    362
363    ORINOCO-VENTUARI CARIB
620393 YABAR  121123226233  92--4101144 2---641212010 1950              363
620452 PANAR  121133226033  96--3101103 4---644200010 1950      750 1954363
620455 MAKIT  121124226033  92--4105004 --4-644200210 1920              363
364    YANOAMA
630723 SANEM  221114216030  90--3145145 -4--841110010 1950     2500    364
365    SHIRIANA
630721 SHIRI  222114256233  99--3125203 -2--641200110 1960     5000 1960365
366    GUIANA CARIB
620189 BCARI  111123226233  91--2121111 2---841211111 1930              366
620450 CAMAR  111132226233  95--4001001 4---441200010 1930              366
620451 MACUS  111133226033  96--4041001 2---641200010 1910              366
```

```
COLS    COLS    COLS      COLS       COLS     COLS   COLS     COLS
1 - 6   7-11    12 - 23   24 - 34    35 - 47  61-64  65 - 73  74 - 80


620454 TAULI 112123226030 92--4241000 2---641000010 1910                    366
630722 WAIWA 111133226233 96--4141041 2---841210110 1950             180 1954366
  367   ORINOCO DELTA
620088 WARRA 221114216033 92--3125233 -4--641002111 1950            8000 1950367
  368   COASTAL ARAWAK
620449 LOCON 112133226030 97--4205111 2---521200010 1900                    368
  369   BUSH NEGROES
620392 SARAM 111133226133 96--4137005 4---721500010 1920                    369
  370   PALIKUR
630292 PALIK 112133226033 95--4121000 1---314000010 1920             240    370
  371   LOWER AMAZON TUPI
630190 TAPIR 112133226133 97--4105243 -1--644122311 1930             149 1939371
690300 TENET 111132225030 07--4115043 -2--641102115 1930            2000    371
  372   MAUE-MUNDURUCU
630090 MUNDU 121123226133 91--4145241 -2--611210310 1950            1250 1952372
630720 MAUE  111132226333 95--4145200 --2-311002010 1950            1400 1958372
  373   SIRIONO-GUARAYU
640091 SIRIO 231114226173 91--3145115 -4--644411111 1940            2000 1940373
  374   PANO
640634 AMAHU 121133226133 95--2151144 ---2441211111 1950                    374
640666 CONIB 112124226033 92--4001144 --4-641010315 1920            1200 1940374
641167 CHACO 111123226233 92--4101001 2---444213310 1960             145 1960374
  375   UPPER AMAZON
641131 COCAM 113123224000 90--4405310 -2--411000110                         375
  376   TUCUNA
640092 TUCUN 112123226133 92--4101212 2---313212211                  3000 1940376
  377   PEBA
640192 YAGUA 131123226073 92--4121142 1---311112111 1940            1000    377
  378   TUCANO
640293 CUBEO 112133226233 96--5241112 2---313203115 1940            2000    378
  379   WITOTO
640347 WITOT 111123226333 92--4241012 2---311213111 1900           15000    379
  380   JIVARO
640191 JIVAR 111132224233 26--2151141 4---241213115 1930            5000 1956380
  381   TUNEBO
650294 TUNEB 111132226233 95--4021213 4---444100110 1950            2000    381
  382   CHIBCHA
650395 CHIBC 111141246030 95--4637440 4---441010010 1540         1000000    382
  383   PAEZ
650348 PAEZ  111131241039 35--2022000 4---244001015 1900                    383
  384   CAYAPA
650194 CAYAP 111132234233 06--2145343 --1-444100115 1910            2000    384
  385   CAMPA
650667 CAMPA 121133226033 96--4141111 2---444300311 1900            5000 1930385
  386   HIGHLAND PERU
650093 INCA  111131242939 371-4704413 1---444320114 1520         5500000    386
  387   AYMARA
650193 AYMAR 111231121933 25--4300333 -1--314111112 1940          600000 1936387
  388   ARAUCANIANS
660195 MAPUC 111131241233 37--2445226 --4-311412112 1880          200000    388
  389   ALACALUF
660396 ALACA 113114256035 99--1151141 2---844301011 1900             200 1900389
  390   YAHGAN
660094 YAHGA 113114256235 99--1151134 2---441112011 1870            2500 1866390
  391   PATAGONIANS
660295 ONA   132114256273 99--1121214 2---444120111 1880            2000    391
660349 TEHUE 131114252170 39--1245211 --2-443312112 1870            1400 1870391
  392   GUAYCURU
670196 ABIPO 131114252273 19--1641041 2---241123011 1800            2000 1767392
670296 CADUV 122114222133 32--1606000 --2-644113111 1940             150 1937392
670724 TOBA  121123232233 01--3142331 --2-844112112 1960           10000 1964392
  393   MASCOI
671168 LENGU 131114216273 93--1145011 -2--644000111 1890            2300 1940393
  394   MATACO
670095 MATAC 112114215233 22--3105244 --2-641112112 1860           20000 1900394
670297 CHORO 221114216233 21--5101144 1---641110112 1910            2500 1915394
```

COLS 1 - 6	COLS 7-11	COLS 12 - 23	COLS 24 - 34	COLS 35 - 47	COLS 61-64	COLS 65 - 73	COLS 74 - 80
395	CHIRIGUANO						
670398	CHIRI	111132226031	17--4046001	--2-441300012	1900		395
396	ZAMUCO						
670397	CHAMA	321114216530	92--1602021	1---641003010	1890		396
397	TERENA						
670096	TEREN	112123221133	01--3645013	-2--844120110	1850	3000	1946397
398	GUATO						
680350	GUATO	212114216333	90--3141000	4---240000310	1900	100	1901398
399	NAMBICUARA						
680198	NAMBI	221114226233	93--3125141	2---444223110	1940	1500	399
400	PARESSI						
681131	PARES	111133226030	00--4245140	-4--644000111	1910	340	1908400
401	BORORO						
680097	BOROR	231114256273	99--3136045	--2-524210011	1920	1000	1936401
681169	UMOTI	111133226231	97--4145243	----444100110	1940	65	1949401
402	BACAIRI						
680197	BACAI	112133226033	95--4125143	--2-444200011	1940	250	1947402
403	CAMAYURA						
680299	CAMAY	112123226233	93--5145211	-2--441200211	1940	110	1948403
404	TRUMAI						
680098	TRUMA	112123226233	91--4245141	-2--444213011	1930	43	1938404
405	CARAJA						
690099	CARAJ	112114226130	93--3245043	--2-644300311	1950	8000	1939405
406	SOUTHERN GE						
690100	SHERE	121123226233	92--4145045	2---314600311	1850	2140	1951406
407	APINAYE-COROA						
690399	APINA	111133226233	95--4135215	-1--5-4122111	1920	160	1937407
690725	COROA	111132226233	95--3135203	1---644123310	1950		407
408	TIMBIRA						
690200	RAMCO	121123224233	22--3105245	--1-521112211	1930	300	1930408
409	GUARANI						
691170	CAYUA	111133226233	97--4001001	1---444000010	1950		409
410	CAINGANG						
690199	AWEIK	231114256279	99--1151143	4---844310110	1910	106	1934410
411	BOTOCUDO						
690299	BOTOC	321114256633	99--1125204	-4--044320010	1880	5100	411
412	COASTAL TUPI						
690400	TUPIN	111123226233	92--4446311	-4--641210015	1600	10000	412

This book was set by photo composition in ten point Baskerville with two points of leading. It was designed and manufactured by Brush-Mill Books, Inc., Chester, Connecticut.